MYSTICISM IN THE WORLD'S RELIGIONS

MYSTICISM

IN THE WORLD'S RELIGIONS

GEOFFREY PARRINDER

Oxford University Press

NEW YORK

First published in Great Britain in 1976
by Sheldon Press

Copyright © 1976 Geoffrey Parrinder
Library of Congress Catalogue Card Number: 76-40554

Printed in the United States of America

The Author

Geoffrey Parrinder is Professor of the Comparative Study of Religions in the University of London. After ordination he spent twenty years teaching in West Africa and studying African religions, and became the founder member of the Department of Religious Studies in the University College of Ibadan, Nigeria. He has travelled widely in Africa, and in India, Pakistan, Sri Lanka, Burma, Iran, Israel, Jordan and Turkey and has lectured in Australia, America and India, and at Oxford. He is the author of many books on world religions which have been translated into eight languages.

CONTENTS

PART I

The Meaning of Mysticism

Chapter 1

INTRODUCTION

There is a widespread modern interest in religious affairs in the broadest sense, from Hare Krishna to the Jesus People and from Transcendental Meditation to the Charismatic Movement. Much of this religious concern does not stop at the traditional borders of religion but penetrates into the mysterious, occult and unfamiliar. There are probably greater varieties of religious experiment today than the Western world has ever known.

Experiment and experience are key words. One may try anything once, and discover by personal involvement whether what the gurus say is true. Religious experience rather than dogma and formal ritual seems to bring life into dull routine, although new movements may have their own dogmatic claims and ordered methods of meditation or worship. Experiment has also led to a search for physical and spiritual exaltation through drugs, music and trance, in attempts to discover higher levels of consciousness.

This variety and experimentation have been greatly extended from the knowledge now available of ancient Eastern religions. This is one of the most significant factors in the religious scene of the twentieth century and it has created a new situation for traditional religion and theology. Serious study of the religions of Asia has been undertaken by Western scholars for about a hundred years, critical books have been written and selections from many scriptures have gradually been published. But for a long time the effect was limited and numbers actively interested were restricted. Small Buddhist or Vedānta societies were founded, and fewer Islamic or Taoist. There were rare centres of worship for visiting Asian ambassadors, traders or students.

In the same period Christian missions were venturing into nearly every country in the world, establishing centres, building schools and disseminating literature. But now the compliment has been returned. Not only visitors but immigrants and missions come from Asia to Europe and America; Gurus and Swamis, Sufis and Dervishes, attract large audiences and often become established teachers of religious experimentation. Meanwhile the disappearance of old political empires has brought decline to some formal structures of the churches and has led to a reassessment of their role and message. The world becomes increasingly unified, religiously as well as commercially or politically, and this brings a shift away from exclusive organizations of former times.

Religious experiment and interest in mystery have led naturally to mysticism. That mystical claims are made in many religions is taken both as proof of the universality of the inner life of the soul and as the real link between religions which may be divided by dogma but are really united in their quest for the universal One. What has been called 'neo-mysticism' is taken to include many diverse forms of experience and exploration.

It follows that mysticism is not now generally thought to be confined to a few athletic heroes of spiritual life, monks in desert cells or yogis on mountain peaks. Mysticism is considered to be more than an esoteric and unusual religious perception, and a recent study of 'inglorious Wordsworths' discovered that there are transcendental experiences in childhood and adolescence among many people even in industrial societies. Mystical experience, it is claimed, is not merely an example and inspiration from the few to the many, but is something in which most people can share.

Yet the variety and all-embracing claims made for mysticism are confusing, and different interpretations given in the world's religions are affected by theological attitudes. This book aims at providing clues to the diverse forms and expressions of mysticism, by considering some of the major religious traditions of East and West. These seem to fall naturally into two principal areas, Monistic and Theistic, though there are minor variations and often overlapping of

INTRODUCTION

these categories. After discussion of the major traditions there is reference to visions, sex and drugs, and a final consideration of the relationship of the expert to the ordinary seeker.

The purpose of this book is to introduce the great religions in their mystical expressions. It does not profess to include all mystics, for even in one religion that would be impossible in one book, but selections are given from many teachers in original versions or from reliable translations, as these throw light on what mystics themselves believe has happened to them. Since it is commonly said that all mysticism is the same or, with equal assurance, that there are quite distinct types, light from mystical teachings themselves may be welcomed even when interpretation is difficult.

This book is an expansion of the Westcott Lectures for 1973 under the Teape Foundation, which were delivered in Delhi and Madras, the first being given under the chairmanship of the Vice-President of India, Dr G. S. Pathak. I am deeply grateful for the honour of being chosen to lecture and for the hospitality of the Principal and staff of St Stephen's College, Delhi, and the directors of the Community Service Centre, Madras. There were discussions in other centres in Delhi, in the University of Madras arranged by Professor T. M. P. Mahadevan, and at the British Institute of Persian Studies in Teheran organized by Professor Hossein Nasr. Earlier that year I lectured on the same theme to the theological faculty of the University of Wales at Bangor, and conversations there and at many other places over the years helped to form views of the nature and variety of mystical experience.

For over forty years I have collected works of mystical authorities from Dionysius to Traherne, and from the Bhagavad Gītā to Jalālu'ddīn Rūmī. In writing other books on religion in Asia and Africa I have often made reference to mystical teachings, but this is my first venture into a full-scale study of the subject. Behind it there is not only reading, discussion and criticism, but personal conviction and experience. The question is often asked, 'Have you had mystical experiences, and what were they?' But one may take refuge in St Paul's statement that he had heard 'unspeakable words, which it is not lawful for a man to utter'. Yet it is strange that mystics, with their unutterable claims, have uttered a great deal. There is a vast

5

literature of mysticism, for mystics are often assertive and state what they hold to be true and real. This truth and reality come out of their own experience, it is practically tested and brings conviction. Therefore what we are engaged in is not merely a detached study or a record of history, but belief and experience which claim to give the final truth about the universe. Mysticism is not a plug for gaps as yet unfilled by science but, on the contrary, its conviction of the mystical unity at the heart of things may alone provide that order and continuity upon which all other studies depend.

Chapter 2

MYSTERY AND UNION

THE MYSTERIES

A Cabbalistic tradition said that mysticism is either a mystery or a mystery of mysteries. It is a mystery when the teacher understands it but the pupil does not, and it is a mystery of mysteries when neither teacher nor pupil understands it.

Many people would agree that mysticism is mysterious, but to identify it with any kind of mystery is not helpful since in popular usage mysticism has been applied to the bizarre or occult. Thus a quality newspaper described a Cambodian general as 'an errant mystic who gauges his major decisions by the devices of fortune-tellers and the paths of the stars'. And the same paper had as its front page headline 'A Mystic and his Mayhem', telling of a Caribbean president whose office was littered with spiritualist magazines but whose police force beat up his opponents.

At a more general level, but still unsatisfactory from a religious point of view, is the opinion that mysticism is vague and unpractical. The *Oxford English Dictionary*, which gives several definitions of mysticism, notes that 'from the hostile point of view, mysticism implies self-delusion or dreamy confusion of thought; hence the term is often applied to any religious belief to which these evil qualities are imputed'. Therefore some old writers referred to the 'trash' or 'poison' of mysticism and others spoke of its vagueness or crude speculations. Recently a writer on mystical experience said that 'seen very broadly, mysticism is a name for our infinite appetites. Less broadly it is the assurance that these appetites can be satisfied.' It

7

may also be an attitude towards 'reality', or even a name for 'the paranoid darkness in which unbalanced people stumble so confidently'.[1]

The origins of the word mysticism were in the Mysteries of ancient Greece. This name was perhaps derived from *muein*, to close the lips or eyes, with the probable primary sense of 'one vowed to keep silence', and hence 'one initiated into the Mysteries'. The Mysteries were secret cults which appear to have been both underground and emotional survivals from pre-Greek religion of the worship of the Earth Mother, which continued under the more formal state ceremonies of Homeric and later times. Similar and parallel movements existed in India where cults of dark gods, like Krishna and the Mother Goddess, seem to have survived the invasion of the Aryan tribes, who were related to the Homeric Greeks, and emerged again to great power in the devotional movements which are still popular.

The Greek Mysteries were associated especially with the Earth Mother, Demeter (the Roman Ceres), and with Dionysus, a god of vegetation and later of wine (hence his other name of Bacchus). The Mysteries at Eleusis, near Athens, celebrated the return of spring and the rising of new corn; commemorated in the story of Persephone (Proserpine), who was rapt away by Pluto to the underworld, ate some pomegranate seeds, was sought by her mother Demeter to return to earth, but went back to Pluto for three months every winter. The ceremonies of the Mysteries are not known in detail, since they were secret, but they included purification by bathing in the sea, initiation, and admission into advanced stages, with perhaps a communion meal and a sacred marriage. The returning life of plants in springtime would symbolize new life for the mystics, associated or united with the deities. Ritual purity and moral righteousness and gentleness were regarded as the fruits of the Mysteries. Dionysiac festivals celebrated agricultural and human fertility in ceremonies from which singing and drama developed.

Both in theory and practice Christianity followed on the ancient Mysteries. Like them, it provided a more personal and emotional religion than the state rituals, and it used terminology associated

[1] A. Scharfstein, *Mystical Experience*, 1973, p. 1.

8

with the Mysteries at Eleusis and elsewhere. As members of a persecuted religion Christians often met in secret, yet their faith was intended to be open to all classes and races, and there was at first no sharp division between the ordinary believer and the mystical expert.

Already in the Apocrypha of the Old Testament a 'mystery' was known to the initiated (*mystes*) as a secret doctrine and this developed into something which, though not necessarily difficult to understand, should not be revealed. In the New Testament the 'mystery' is the revelation of the word of God, which had not been known in previous ages but was now revealed to believers. 'Behold, I tell you a mystery', said Paul in such a sense. But Paul used other terms which could have a technical mystical association, such as 'illuminated', 'fullness', 'perfect' and 'wisdom'. 'We speak wisdom among the perfect', he says, and 'we speak God's wisdom in a mystery' (1 Cor. 2.6–7). Paul wrote of his own mystical vision as being 'caught up to the third heaven' and hearing unspeakable words (2 Cor. 12.1–4).

Early Christian writers developed biblical teachings and freely borrowed terminology from the Mysteries. In the second century Clement of Alexandria wrote of 'the mysteries of the Word'. Christ was the 'Teacher of the divine mysteries' into which the Christian convert would be 'initiated', and with advanced teaching he would proceed to 'the great mysteries'. Other theologians spoke regularly of the sacraments as *mysteria*, baptism as *mystikon*, and the celebrants of the eucharistic mystery were 'mystagogues'.

While Christian teachers, such as Clement and Origen, were developing systems of thought and using both biblical and traditional Greek ideas and expressions, there was a profound development of Greek thought itself. This was in the Neoplatonism of Plotinus and his followers. Plato has been regarded as the greatest of all philosophers, in due course being taken into both Christian and Islamic philosophy, and his influence remains to this day. But Plotinus welded Platonic and other mystical ideas into a coherent whole and his essays are among the classics of mysticism. Plotinus taught the union (*enosis*) of the soul with the divine one, which is the Good and the source of all existence and values.

As Christian writers absorbed Neoplatonic ideas a crucial role was played by the short but potent writings of the so-called Dionysius, probably an anonymous Syrian monk who lived about A.D. 500. Dionysius used many technical terms of the Mysteries and he presented Christian teaching as a synthesis with Neoplatonism.

In his *Ecclesiastical Hierarchies* Dionysius expounds three ways of spiritual life by which human nature is 'divinized'. These are purgation, illumination and union, the three stages of mystical progress which appear in the teachings of many later Christian mystics and which were already suggested by the three stages of perfection taught by Plotinus.

Since God is himself a mystery, and cannot be fully known by finite man, negative as well as positive assertions are made about him. Dionysius taught a negative way of mystical effort, wherein the mystic is plunged into the 'Darkness of Unknowing' and is 'wholly absorbed in him who is beyond all'. In his *Mystical Theology* he writes of the mystic way ascending from the particular to the universal, venturing beyond all the positive divine attributes, so that 'without a veil, we may know that Unknowing which is shrouded under everything that is known or can be known, and that we may contemplate that superessential Darkness which is hidden by the light that is in existing things'.[2]

Dionysius, like Plotinus, wrote of the 'union' of the soul with God, and of the gradual 'divinization' (*theosis*) of man. He says that by the exercise of mystical contemplation the mystic will rise 'by unknowing' (*agnosia*) towards the union, as far as it is attainable, with him who 'transcends all being and knowledge'.

This mystical a-gnosticism, un-knowing, influenced some writers more than others, and it had an interesting echo later in English mystical treatises, such as the anonymous fourteenth-century work *The Cloud of Unknowing*, to which we shall come. For the moment it may suffice to fix upon the concept of 'union', which appears plainly in Plotinus and Dionysius, which had previously been present under other terms, and which becomes characteristic of a great deal of mystical thought.

[2] Dionysius, *Mystical Theology*, Chapters 1–2.

MYSTERY AND UNION

Two major definitions of mysticism given in the dictionary need consideration. First, it is said to be 'reliance on spiritual intuition or exalted feeling as the means of acquiring knowledge of mysteries inaccessible to intellectual apprehension'. This does not necessarily mean that mystics discover new facts, for that is the role of science, but that they seek a wisdom which gives a new vision and understanding of the world. This is how William Blake expressed it:

> To see a World in a Grain of Sand
> And a Heaven in a Wild Flower,
> Hold Infinity in the palm of your hand
> And Eternity in an hour.

Mystics have often spoken in poetical ways, and some have been chaotic. But a modern philosopher claims that there is a 'logic of mysticism', so that 'ultimately there may prove to be only one such satisfactory pattern of consistency or logicality, and that a mystical one'. Far from being abnormal or irrelevant, the discovery of a mystical unity at the heart of things is the true knowledge that gives meaning to our daily work.[3]

In another important study of mysticism, by the philosopher W. T. Stace, a search was made for a 'universal core' of mystical expression. Seven representative experiences were chosen: two Roman Catholic, one Protestant, one ancient classical, one modern Hindu, and two American agnostic. From their statements central themes were selected and set out in seven propositions:

1. There is a unifying vision, in which the One is perceived by the senses in and through many objects, so that 'All is One'.

2. The One is apprehended as an inner life, or presence in all things, so that 'nothing is really dead'.

3. This brings a sense of reality, which is objective and true.

4. There is a feeling of satisfaction, joy and bliss.

5. There is a feeling of the holy and sacred, which is the specifically religious element of the experience.

6. There is a feeling that it is paradoxical.

[3] J. N. Findlay, *Ascent to the Absolute*, 1970, p. 179.

11

7. There is a feeling that it is inexpressible in words.[4]

These propositions have been criticized from different sides. They are said to be too vague, or too inclusive. They have been called a ragbag of single cases without a clear unity, and on the other hand they are said to be too synthetic and not taking account of different forms of mystical belief or expression.

This supposed 'universal core' of mysticism does not tell us much about the content of mystical experience, which to mystics is the central concern. Feelings are emphasized, and a unifying vision of an inner life, but it is not clear in what the object of the mystical vision consists, apart from the One where apparently all is one. Yet it is here that differences of mystical doctrine, and perhaps of mystical experience, are most clear. Stace seems to suggest that the quintessence of mysticism is the One, a kind of pantheism, or more strictly monism (the belief that there exists only one universal being). Yet there are other kinds of mystical understanding, as further study will show. The notion that mysticism is essentially monistic, having its perfect exposition in the Indian Upanishads, and that all other kinds of mysticism are inferior, is quite common nowadays but it is contradicted by eminent mystics from other schools of thought.

This leads to further consideration of mysticism in terms of union. The dictionary gives its central definition of mysticism as 'belief in the possibility of union with the Divine nature by means of ecstatic contemplation', and it further defines a mystic as 'one who, whether Christian or non-Christian, seeks by contemplation or self-surrender to obtain union with or absorption into the Deity'. But this definition could not include a Buddhist, who believes in no supreme deity but may claim to be a mystic, and the dictionary definition here is not so wide as its later statement on worship, which is described as 'reverence or veneration paid to a being or power regarded as supernatural or divine'. A Buddhist would not object to that, though consideration must be given in due course to the particular nature of Buddhist mysticism.

Some of the most important contributions to an understanding of different types of mysticism have been made by R. C. Zaehner who, until his death in 1974, was Spalding Professor of Eastern Religions

[4] W. T. Stace, *Mysticism and Philosophy*, 1960, p. 79.

and Ethics in Oxford University.[5] His treatment of mysticism has been admired and criticized, but it should not be ignored; he is highly critical of those writers who would reduce all mystical experience to the same level, high or low, and he formulates his own definitions of different types of mysticism.

Basic to the idea of mysticism is union, but not only are there different kinds of union, there are also different understandings of the object with which union is achieved. What Zaehner terms 'profane mysticism' is that which may speak of union simply as 'all is one', a feeling of oneness but without any divine or religious object. Aldous Huxley took the drug mescalin in a famous series of experiments and used religious language to describe his experiences, but his explanation was simply that of oneness. He said that by contemplating the legs of a chair he actually *became* them, 'not merely gazing at those bamboo legs but actually *being* them'.[6] He also spoke of his experience as the Beatific Vision, in both Christian and Indian terms, but since he did not describe this in any clear way or indicate its content his language may have been exaggerated. As with some nature mystics, though not all, there was an expression of unity without any clear content.

The simple experience of unification has sometimes been termed Pantheism, but that may be a mistake. Pan-theism is the doctrine that God, or at least the divine being, is everything and everything is divine. But a simple feeling of unity or exaltation does not necessarily involve any divine being or *theos*. It can be expressed by a phrase from the Upanishads, 'You are this all', but that has no evident reference to any divine being. Zaehner prefers to call such a simple expression of unity Pan-en-henism, 'all-in-one-ism'. It is profane, not in any derogatory sense, but simply because no sacred power is implied.

There is a pantheistic mysticism, however, which may be called 'all-God-ism'. This is illustrated by famous sayings of the Upanishads such as 'Thou art That' and 'I am Brahman'. These expressions mean that the individual soul is the eternal and only real Absolute, the ultimate Being. This has often been called Pantheism

[5] R. C. Zaehner, *Mysticism Sacred and Profane*, 1957.
[6] Aldous Huxley, *The Doors of Perception*, 1954, pp. 15 f.

by Western writers, but it may be questioned whether such belief really implies a mystical union, since according to the theory of the Absolute (Brahman) this is the only truly existent being. One is not united to Brahman, one is it.

'In Christian terminology', says Zaehner, 'mysticism means union with God; in non-theistical contexts it also means union with some principle or other.'[7] This is true not only of Christians but of all mystics who believe in some kind of God, Muslims, Jews, theistic Hindus and the like. Ideas of God differ greatly and the 'personal' nature of God may be variously defined. But theistic mysticism is certainly a major and historical form of this experience. On the other hand an assertion of mere unity, whether of the natural or the monistic variety, may be difficult to discuss. To affirm the identity of subject and object is to say that whatever is is, existence exists. It is tautology, since a valid description implies distinction, and relationship requires difference. We shall find many examples of the need to give personal expression to abstract relationship. The achievement of union, as in a marriage, means that there was formerly separation, yet even when the two become 'one flesh' some differences remain; *vive la différence!*

Christian mystics have often spoken of being united with God and we have seen that Dionysius wrote of the divinization of man, but here there are subtle distinctions. Some later mystics spoke of being 'deified', but they generally thought that there remained some difference between divine and human in this unity. Broadly the distinction is between unity and identity, or between theism and monism. To say 'Abide in me and I in you' (John 15.4) is the closest divine-human union, though in the context of this passage the vine and the branches are differentiated. Certainly this is not the identity which could say 'I am you and you are me'. Christian and Jewish mystics do not say 'I am God', even in their closest search for union or partaking of the divine nature. Some Muslim mystics have seemed to dare so far, though even when Hallāj said 'I am the Real' or 'the Truth', he did not claim 'I am Allah'.

Monistic Hindus declared 'I am Brahman', yet Brahman is not God in the sense of a personal theism but a pervading principle.

[7] R. C. Zaehner, *Mysticism Sacred and Profane*, p. 32.

Theistic works, like the Hindu Bhagavad Gītā ('The Song of the Blessed One', that is, Krishna, who is here the sole deity) never say 'I am God', or even use the Upanishadic phrase 'Thou art That'. Krishna in the Gītā says:

> All this cosmos is pervaded
> by Me in form Unmanifest;
> in Me all beings must subsist
> although in them I never rest.[8]

When Krishna identifies himself with the best in every class of being he even says that he is Arjuna his hearer. But the opposite is never stated, Arjuna is not God even when he is in the closest loving relationship with him.

It is not easy to find an Indian term to correspond to the European word mysticism, in the sense of union, but the closest is probably Yoga. This ancient and complex word has at its origin a meaning of joining or harnessing, and it is directly related to the English word 'yoke'. Although Yoga is used in a great variety of ways, and notably in the Bhagavad Gītā, where there are many subtle shifts of the meaning of the word, the unification or integration of personality is one great aim of Yoga. The other major aim is union with God. These distinct forms of Yoga will be discussed later.

In Islamic mysticism also a central term that reflects the concern of other theistic mysticisms is unity. This is *tawhīd*, which means making one or asserting oneness. It is applied to the unity of God, who is oneness in himself, but in mystical terminology it indicates the union of the human personality with the divine. Here again there were qualifications between unity and identity, or between communion with God and pantheism, and these will be considered in the appropriate chapter.

We conclude for the moment with this distinction of different types of mysticism. Theistic mysticism seeks union with God but not identity. Monistic mysticism seeks identity with a universal principle, which may be called divine though that would imply a difference from the human. Non-religious mysticism also seeks union with something, or everything, rather like monism. How mysticism

---

[8] Bhagavad Gītā, 9.4; see also 10.37.

appears in different guises in various religious and non-religious traditions will be our concern in the following chapters. Clearly this cannot be a complete account of world mysticism, or even the full detail of the mysticism of one religion, but it is hoped to introduce and discuss some of the important features and problems of mysticism in what William James, the American psychologist, called the 'Varieties of Religious Experience'.

PART II

Mystical Monism

Chapter 3

NATURAL PANTHEISM

UNIVERSALITY

Mysticism as a search for unity has been described in many ages and religions, so that it is practically universal. The mystic, furthermore, may be the expert, differing in degree from the ordinary believer by the intensity or frequency of his mystical visions, but he need not be different in kind, since the layman has some spiritual awareness. In this sense mysticism may be called natural, since it appears to be common to mankind, to be part of human nature.

Such a statement may raise the question whether mystical experiences are genuine or should be accepted as such. Believers would protest that at least their own experiences are true, and perhaps that some others may have them, or at least that religion has a life of its own independently of the social or psychological environment. Those many people today who are seeking new forms of spiritual illumination, by drugs, music or new religious movements, would hold that the experience is its own justification and that one cannot share in another's experience. Yet it is also true that environment, group, tradition, materials used, and so on, should all be examined in relationship to the claimed experience, and the value of a community is that it serves as a check upon extravagant claims. 'I would rather speak five words with my mind, in order to instruct others, than ten thousand words in tongues', said Paul (1 Cor. 14.19).

An eminent social anthropologist, who writes as an agnostic, recognizes that full credit must be given to the mystic's own account

19

of his experiences, which are genuine for him. 'It is not suggested that such beliefs should be dismissed as figments of the disordered imaginations of credulous peoples. For those who believe in them, mystical powers are realities both of thought and experience.'[1] Moreover he refuses to follow some other anthropologists who think that spiritual beliefs are so absurd that people cannot really believe in them. Since they patently do so the phenomena must be studied on their own terms.

There are difficulties, however, for believers in understanding accounts of experiences given by those who express them in the terminology of another religion. Can a believer in Allah understand a follower of Tao? What has Athens to do with Jerusalem? To the monotheist mystical experiences are a gift of God, an act of grace, an original divine initiative which may be peculiar to his own special revelation. To the pantheist or monist they are experiences of the One, which is identical with himself, and which is probably the same in all religions and even in secular mysticism. In face of this easy-going tolerance or indifferentism it is perhaps not surprising that monotheists are often intolerant, believing that God has chosen them and by implication not others. Yet they would do well to follow the open-mindedness of the agnostic anthropologist and give others credit for their claims to have mystical experiences. And theologically it may be more sound to hold that God works in mysterious and diverse ways, even if we cannot understand his purposes. God may be thought to have spoken to a pantheist who does not recognize a personal deity, and his experience should not be denied by someone who has not had that experience. A genuine monotheist may not believe that all mystical experiences are the same, or that it does not matter how they are interpreted, and yet he can hold to his belief that the 'unknown Christ' in another religion is the 'known Christ' in his own.[2]

Not only are mystical experiences universal and pertaining to man's religious nature, they are also claimed to have been inspired by the visible world, by Nature. In modern times a great deal has been made of Nature Mysticism and many people have had experiences of

[1] I. M. Lewis, *Ecstatic Religion*, 1971, p. 28.
[2] R. Panikkar, *The Unknown Christ of Hinduism*, 1964, pp. 45 f.

exaltation or ecstasy inspired by natural settings or events, but can they truly be called mystical? Is there unity, and is it connected with a pantheistic or a theistic interpretation?

One of the favourite writers on nature mysticism was W. H. Hudson in *Far Away and Long Ago*. Among many absorbing passages he wrote of an 'animism' which is:

> the sense and apprehension of an intelligence like our own but more powerful in all visible things. It persists and lives in many of us, I imagine, more than we like to think, or more than we know, especially in those born and bred amidst rural surroundings. . . . This faculty or instinct of the dawning mind is or has always seemed to me essentially religious in character; undoubtedly it is the root of all nature-worship, from fetishism to the highest pantheistic development.[3]

Such apprehensions of an intelligent presence are not rare or out of date. In 1973 a researcher asked schoolchildren and undergraduates whether they had had any experiences like those described by Hudson sixty years ago, and of the four hundred questioned over half replied that they had. Many young people described experiences in the evening, or at some beauty spot, which brought wonder, awe and peace. The appeal of such experiences is similar to that which others have found in Eastern teachings or yogic practices, and which others have sought in drugs.[4]

But that such feelings may not necessarily be religious or theistic is suggested by Marghanita Laski's writings on *Ecstasy*.[5] Here she is more concerned with the phenomena of feelings, transcendent elevation or ecstasy than with mystical union. But feelings are aroused by many different physical and mental states and contacts, and something more than feeling should be considered. In her research Miss Laski questioned sixty-three people of her acquaintance over a period of three years and sixty gave affirmative answers to the question, 'Do you know a sensation of transcendent

[3] W. H. Hudson, *Far Away and Long Ago*. Many editions since 1918, ch. 17.

[4] M. Paffard, *Inglorious Wordsworths*, 1973.

[5] Marghanita Laski, *Ecstasy*, 1961, pp. 9, 526, and lectures at King's College, London, 1974.

ecstasy?' They were asked how many times this experience had occurred, what had induced it, how it could be described, and what their religion was. She describes herself as an agnostic and so were some of her witnesses. So that while for some what were called the causes or 'triggers' of ecstasy were religion, for others they were art, music, nature, and so on.

Admittedly these friends were middle-class intellectuals, and therefore an appendix was added on a questionnaire which had been sent to people in 'a working-class district of London'. Forms were sent through the post to a hundred people, of whom only eleven replied in the enclosed stamped addressed envelopes. The others probably threw them away or steamed off the stamps. The question was simplified for this audience and read, 'Have you ever known a feeling of unearthly ecstasy?' Only one correspondent admitted to this, and he was 'a newspaper-packer whose age was over fifty' who claimed to be a rationalist. But perhaps the others did not know what was meant by 'unearthly ecstasy', since although ten of them answered No to the first question they filled in all the factual details required.

Such experiments do not give much information on mystical union, and perhaps some of them were not mystical, but some negative conclusion may be suggested by Miss Laski's research. Religion was called 'the opiate of the masses' by Karl Marx, and even I. M. Lewis suggests that ecstatic religion appears more frequently under 'the pressure of adverse circumstances'. But Miss Laski's middle-class friends were neither deprived nor repressed, and it was the working-class inquiry, in so far as it was conducted, which gave much lower results. Are the working classes now irreligious, in London at least? And is the ecstatic, and perhaps mystical, experience becoming rarer? Such questions cannot be answered without much fuller research, which would, as W. H. Hudson would have agreed, consider the effect of urban and industrial environment on the human spirit. Further, the whole world and all religions must be taken into account. Perhaps the nature of man is better developed in his natural environment than in artificial and depressing surroundings. Or perhaps religious enthusiasm has been diverted into football orgies or obsession with television. But more must be said now of the character of nature mysticism as such.

NATURAL PANTHEISM

In the opera *Patience* W. S. Gilbert wrote:

> You must lie upon the daisies, and discourse in
>   novel phrases of your complicated state of mind.
> The meaning doesn't matter if it's only idle chatter
>   of a transcendental kind.
>   And everyone will say
>   As you walk your mystic way,
> If this young man expresses himself in terms
>   too deep for *me*,
> Why, what a very singularly deep young man
>   this deep young man must be!

Other critics of nature mysticism have attacked the concentration upon feelings of ecstasy and declared that whatever else they may be they are not mystical. It is not enough to lie in the grass on a warm summer's day and feel transfused with joy, but is this a mystical sense of union with either God or the One? R. C. Zaehner goes further, and in an attempt to isolate 'strictly religious mysticism', including Hindu, Christian and Muslim, he firmly excludes nature mysticism since he considers that mysticism necessarily implies exclusion of the world:

> The whole purpose of the exercise is to concentrate on an ultimate reality to the complete exclusion of all else; and by all 'else' is meant the phenomenal world. . . . The exclusion of all that we commonly call Nature is the *sine qua non* of this type of mystical experience: it is the necessary prelude to the further experience of union with God.[6]

But the claim for a 'total and absolute detachment from Nature' may be questioned, first by considering the role played by nature among a wide range of undoubtedly religious mystics. Thomas Traherne said:

> The Earth, the Seas, the Light, the lofty Skies
> The Sun and Stars are mine . . .

[6] R. C. Zaehner, *Mysticism Sacred and Profane*, p. 33.

23

and he cherished them as 'a Gift from God'.[7] But nature mysticism is not merely a northern European and American phenomenon, a product of WASPS (White Anglo-Saxon Protestants), for the stimulus of nature has been widespread and agelong, ranging as far as Chinese Tao and Japanese Shinto.

Many religious mystics have found God through nature and have not fled from it. The visitor to Domrémy today, if he stays overnight when the tourists and coaches have gone and the modern basilica is closed, may be impressed by the quiet of the country, the open plains and gentle hills of Champagne where Joan of Arc lived in the fifteenth century. Joan claimed to hear supernatural voices and they seem appropriate in this setting. A similar feeling may come at Assisi, on the hillsides above the Umbrian plains, where Francis heard God calling him to rebuild his church and from where he went out into the world and embraced a leper.

It was in the hills outside Mecca that Muhammad received his first revelations. The Prophet loved solitude and he would pray in seclusion on Mount Hira and then return to give alms to the poor. On the way to the mountain the very stones and trees saluted him as the apostle of God and then the Qur'ān was revealed, 'and it was peace till the break of day'. Many times in later life Muhammad rose in the night or went aside during the day to the quiet of nature where he believed God spoke to him.

And may not much be said of the natural environment of Galilee, not for its separation from the world but as the setting for mystical experience? Nazareth today is a noisy place of large shrines and bustling shops, but on the open hills where fields run down to the Sea of Galilee there are still black Bedouin tents, and with birds singing in the quiet morning air it is not difficult to make an imaginative return over two thousand years. It was Jesus who spoke of union with the Father but also referred to the birds of the air, the lilies in the field, the sower on the hillside, the seed growing in secret, the red sky at night, the power of the storm and the calm of the wilderness.

Nature has been important in theistic as well as in pantheistic mysticism, and the world-denial of some forms of mysticism, which will be considered later, is paralleled by the world-affirmation of

[7] T. Traherne, *The Salutation.*

others. Perhaps when the population of the world was smaller and man lived closer to nature, mystical experience may have come through more easily than in modern cities, and the popularity of nature mysticism in the Western world may be a reaction against the artificiality of ways of living which cut man off from his natural roots.

Nature mysticism has been attacked in the assumption that identification with nature is the same as union with God, though many writers do not make such an identification. There are different forms of mysticism and among these nature mysticism should find a place. But attack has been directed at the high priests of English nature poetry, Wordsworth and Blake, no doubt with the aim of suggesting that if these can be shown to be unmystical then lesser writers can be ruled out entirely.

Wordsworth's *Tintern Abbey* is a favourite source of quotation, and some of the most moving lines have often been claimed as mystical:

> And I have felt
> A presence that disturbs me with the joy
> Of elevated thoughts; a sense sublime
> Of something far more deeply interfused,
> Whose dwelling is the light of setting suns,
> And the round ocean, and the living air,
> And the blue sky, and in the mind of man:
> A motion and a spirit, that impels
> All thinking things, all objects of all thought,
> And rolls through all things.

But Zaehner claims that here there is little more than an intimation of something which informs and transcends nature, and 'there is no trace of an actual experience at all'.[8] This is astonishing, since Wordsworth said specifically 'I have felt', and to suspect that there is 'no communion with God' here ignores the vital clauses, 'a presence that disturbs me' and 'a spirit, that impels all thinking things'.

Wordsworth's reputation as a mystic does not rest on one poem,

---

[8] R. C. Zaehner, *Mysticism Sacred and Profane*, p. 35.

and in the *Intimations of Immortality* he uses words that might seem almost Indian:

> Our birth is but a sleep and a forgetting.

But he goes on to theism by showing the divine origin of the soul:

> But trailing clouds of glory do we come
> From God, who is our home.

In his earlier years Wordsworth was not an orthodox Christian and his later *Ecclesiastical Sketches* are often tedious but his search for reality inspired a variety of mystical expressions. Far from not showing a trace of actual experience, one of his longest poems, *The Prelude*, is subtitled 'Growth of a Poet's Mind; an Autobiographical Poem', and here it is experience, through nature, of communion with the divine being.

> I felt the sentiment of Being spread
> O'er all that moves and all that seemeth still . . .
> Communing in this sort through earth and heaven
> With every form of creature, as it looked
> Towards the Uncreated with a countenance
> Of Adoration, with an eye of love. (2, 401–2, 411–14)

Wordsworth speaks plainly of 'Nature and her overflowing soul', but he affirms that his experience is 'with God and Nature communing', and in his affirmation of the adoration and love that all creatures have for the Uncreated he comes very close to that more personal mysticism which so often arises like a lotus from the pool of pantheism. Again and again in the history of religions ardent devotion reacted against blank monism. 'I became ever more attached to the Absolute made personal', said the sixteenth-century Indian mystic Tulsī Dās.[9] One cannot adore the impersonal, and the 'eye of love' of which Wordsworth wrote must be directed towards the God with whom he ends his poem (14.205).

William Blake is described on his memorial tablet in St Paul's cathedral as 'artist, poet, mystic', yet this has been questioned. But Blake read and quoted many mystical writers from Plotinus to

[9] W. D. P. Hill, *The Holy Lake of the Acts of Rāma*, 1952, p. 484.

Boehme and Swedenborg, and the theme of his *Book of Thel* is Neoplatonic, using the idea of the descent of the soul into the world. But especially in *Jerusalem, the Emanation of the Giant Albion*, Blake uses mystical language. He speaks of himself and his reader being 'wholly One in Jesus our Lord', using marriage union symbolism in 'the Lamb of God and fair Jerusalem his Bride', beginning with man 'in the Bosom of God', and ending with 'All Human Forms identified. . . . Awaking into his Bosom in the Life of Immortality.'

Blake was admittedly a superb poet and painter, but perhaps the arts have no necessary connection with mysticism. Yet it can be no accident that so much mystical writing is also great poetry or prose, and it springs from an inner concordance of art and religion, a similar mystical vision. Most of the classical Upanishads are in verse, and so are the Bhagavad Gītā and countless later Hindu mystical and devotional works. The great Sufi mystics were often great poets, such as Rūmī, Hallāj, Hāfiz and even Omar Khayyām. Not only Blake and Wordsworth, but the English metaphysical poets and moderns like Hopkins and Eliot have been claimed as mystical.

Another criticism of nature mysticisms is that they do not appear to be 'connected with contemplative techniques', nor are their experiences an interior kind of vision, but 'they occur with the eyes open'.[10] Wordsworth is given again as an example, but we have suggested that his experience was far more than an outward picture and it brought a certainty of eternal things. If he practised no formal or traditional religious techniques, it is clear that for many years Wordsworth sought with mental and spiritual concentration his intimations of immortality.

A further criticism is that the vision of the nature mystic does not correspond to the formless void of the Indian contemplative or the obscurity of *The Cloud of Unknowing*, but it is not clear why it should do so and why it should be 'reasonable to neglect' nature mysticism.[11] The experiences of the nature mystic may, or may not, be similar to those of pantheistic or theistic mystics, but it would be generally agreed that nature mysticism is important, and it shows

[10] N. Smart, *The Yogi and the Devotee*, 1968, pp. 66 f.
[11] Ibid., p. 67.

variations which correspond to those in other forms of mystical experience.

NATURE AND GOD

A distinction may be drawn, however, between nature mystics who feel some harmony with nature or a vague principle, and those who are led into a more theistic form. W. H. Hudson, and even more Richard Jefferies (in *The Story of My Heart*, 1883), who held that 'there is no god in nature', may be classed among those who sought communion with earth and sky but felt no more. But we have seen that Wordsworth's 'being' and 'spirit' led him to God, and Blake has been called 'God-possessed', which is a good description of a theistic mystic.

Other poets have turned deliberately away from nature because they felt its character to be so different from man that it could not help him. In his famous and romantic *Hound of Heaven* Francis Thompson described his disillusionment with nature because of its different language or silence.

> Nature, poor stepdame, cannot slake my drouth;
>   Let her, if she would owe me,
> Drop yon blue bosom-veil of sky, and show me
>   The breasts o' her tenderness:
> Never did any milk of hers once bless
>   My thirsting mouth.

So Thompson waited for the following feet of the personal divine lover, the God who first sought him and to whom he was finally united in love. It was the lack of love that proved the barrenness of nature; for all its charms it was basically heartless and had not even any comforting breasts. A modern scientist might say that we misinterpret nature by trying to fit it into our own categories, and a theist would add that we need to look beyond nature to the divine Being, both immanent in nature and transcendent over it.

Coleridge had a similar thought, speaking of nature not as Wordsworth had taught him but from his own bitter experience:

It were a vain endeavour,
Though I should gaze for ever
On that green light that lingers in the west:
I may not hope from outward forms to win
The passion and the life, whose fountains are within.[12]

Most of these poets and writers about nature had some Christian or theistic background. Hudson wrote at length on his childhood Christian training, and although later he spoke of 'animism' it was of 'an intelligence like our own', and for Wordsworth it was 'a spirit, that impels all thinking things'. An anthropomorphic idea of God may have been refined into the Uncreated, but it is a Being and not an abstraction. It is not mere nature either, in the sense of plain rock and water, that inspires most nature mystics, but the Being within and beyond, as Coleridge and Thompson clearly saw.

Just as in polytheism it is not the solar disc or the vault of heaven but the indwelling spirits that are worshipped, just as 'the heathen in his blindness' does not bow down to wood and stone but reveres the power behind material objects, so most nature mystics seek for communion with that 'presence that disturbs me with the joy of elevated thoughts'. This may be pantheistic or theistic, but it is mysticism, it is a communion which may claim unity or even identity with the divine.

[12] S. T. Coleridge, 'Dejection', III.

Chapter 4

INDIAN PHILOSOPHICAL MONISM

WORLD-DENIAL

Indian mysticism is often taken as the prime example but it is very diverse. Differently from the nature mysticism of the West or Far East, there is a strong element of world-denial and yet there is world-affirmation also. There is both monism and theism, at many different periods.

The earliest documents of Hindu religion are the hymns of the Vedas, which are generally world-affirming, concerned with well-being on this earth. Their experiences of the divine express the power and the presence of the supernatural over and within nature. Only occasionally do we read of the long-haired silent one (*muni*) into whom the gods enter and who flies through the air on the winds (Rig Veda 10.36). Such individuals may, or may not, be connected with the proto-Yogi figures which are depicted on a few surviving stone seals from the Indus Valley civilization, from before 1500 B.C. Belief that certain men can fly is found in many lands and times; some Yogis had long hair and others shaved it off; the Yogic cross-legged posture suggests calm meditation rather than ecstatic flight.

In later times the statements of the Vedas, which had often been expressions of mystical experiences, degenerated into ritual repetition and bargaining with the deities. Yet while in repeating hymns and sacrifices there was much of what, to a critical outsider, might appear to be unproductive effort, and so other-worldly, most of their concerns were material and moral. Similar matters appear constantly in popular religious activities in both ancient and later

30

times, when religion was a central part of life and inspired every action.

World-denial appears in Indian thought and practice, alongside world-affirmation, and it developed gradually. After the Vedas came the Brāhmanas, ritual texts for the Brahmin priests, and the Aranyakas, 'forest treatises' for those who went apart from the world. These were followed by the more systematic Upanishads, 'sessions' which overlap the previous texts so that the first of them is called the Great Forest Upanishad. From early settlements of the Aryan invaders on the plains of the Indus river and its tributaries, the subjugation and also mingling of older peoples, there developed over a thousand years more orderly societies, spreading down the Ganges plains. With the growth of towns and cities there was leisure for speculative thought, the formation of schools of doctrine and meditation, and some reaction against city life towards the peace of the forest.

By the time of the Upanishads, about 600 B.C., there were many ascetics, and religious and philosophical teachings were propagated by such men as well as by priests who continued to repeat sacrifices and formulas. Such ascetics were called 'forest-dwellers' (vāna-prastha), but the word forest was used in a loose fashion since any uncultivated land could be called forest. Some ascetics were heroic world-renouncers who lived in the heart of the jungle or on rough mountain peaks, suffering from cold and heat, hunger and thirst, dangers from animals and even more from insects. Others lived near towns in 'penance-grounds' where they tortured themselves by hanging upside down from trees, sitting near blazing fires, lying on beds of spikes, gazing at the sun, or holding their arms in the air till they withered up. Some of these were earnest men who sought spiritual ecstasy and enlightenment, and others were perhaps psychopaths. Both kinds have survived to this day and in the popular mind these are the true ascetics or mystics.

Many other ascetics, however, were less severe in world-denial, though they might retire to the quiet of nature at times. Some lived by themselves not far from towns and others formed communities. Some wandered from village to village teaching their doctrines and maintaining them in argument, while others established schools where teacher and pupil engaged in dialogue in a true Upanishad, which means literally 'to sit-down-near' a teacher.

Such teachers were the experts in philosophical teaching or ascetic and mystical experience, but in the normal life of the ordinary Hindu there was an ascetic stage. Three or four stages of life were traditionally laid down for the initiated or twice-born Hindu, and these were both worldly and unworldly. He began as a student of sacred knowledge, became a married householder, and only when he had seen the birth of his grandsons, to ensure ritual offerings to the ancestral spirits, would he retire to the forest. He became a forest-dweller either alone or accompanied by his wife. At a later stage he might become a complete renouncer and make his way to a holy place like Benares to await death in meditation. Many forest-dwellers had a wife or disciples to care for them and 'a village nearby for support'.

World-denial should be studied not simply in the way of life or degree of asceticism, but in the teaching of important thinkers. The first Upanishad says that men who seek the Soul in all things have passed beyond hunger and thirst, sorrow and delusion, age and death.

> Those who know the Soul renounce the desire for sons or wealth or possessions and live as beggars. For to desire sons is to desire wealth and this is to desire possessions, and all of these are merely desires. So a man should be disgusted with learning and live as a child, and when he is disgusted with both learning and childishness he becomes a silent sage. And when he is disgusted with both asceticism and non-asceticism, he becomes a true sage.[1]

A few other examples of world-renunciation are given but it is remarkable that the Upanishads, which are often regarded as mystical treatises, have very few autobiographical details, and the experiences upon which they seem to be founded have to be deduced from their teachings. There is a search for mystical unity, but it is expressed in dogmatic statement rather than in described experience.

---

[1] Brihad-āranyaka Upanishad, 3.5.

INDIAN PHILOSOPHICAL MONISM

MONISTIC MYSTICISM

The Vedas speak of many gods though there are developments towards either a henotheism, in which one god is regarded as supreme for his particular worshipper, or a monism in which 'that One' is seen as beyond all else. It is recognized that different gods are named, but 'That which is One the sages call by many names.' And a famous hymn of creation speculates about what there was in the beginning:

> Then there was neither existence nor non-existence . . .
> There was that One and no other,
> The One breathed without breath, self-sustaining.[2]

The philosophical treatises of the Upanishads provide the earliest extensive and systematic works of Indian philosophy. They are both monistic and mystical in parts, but not exclusively. Their dialogues introduce a rational element which has had a long tradition in India, and which could later be turned to the service of social and political problems.

The Upanishads, like other philosophies and science, look for unifying principles in the universe. They try to explain the world in elemental terms, emphasizing especially power, breath and, surprisingly, food. One well-known Upanishad affirms that the cosmic Being, Brahman, 'is food'. For food, as living matter, is the basis of life upon which breath depends, as well as mind, understanding and bliss. Hence matter and spirit are bound together in a mysticism of union with the whole of existence, which is a participation in rather than a withdrawal from the world. So the Upanishadic mystic cries out in ecstasy, in one of the rare personal statements:

> Wonderful! Wonderful! Wonderful!
> I am food! I am food! I am food!
> I am an eater of food . . .
> I am a maker of verses . . .
> I am first of the world-order,

[2] Rig Veda, 10.129.

I am earlier than the gods . . .
I, who am food, eat the eater of food!
I have overcome the whole world![3]

The Upanishads seek for a single principle as the changeless ground of the universe. Sometimes this is the soul or self (*ātman*), both particular and universal. When the sage Yājña-valkya was leaving his wife to go forth to the forest-dwelling stage of life he offered her a settlement. She asked whether this would make her immortal and if not what could achieve that. He replied that only 'love of the soul' could make anything dear, enumerating husband, wife, sons and all possessions.

It is the Soul that should be seen, heard, thought about and considered, for by understanding the Soul all the universe is known.[4]

Another term used in the Upanishads is Brahman, which at first meant power and developed into sacred power, universal spirit, world-ground, the All, cosmic Being.

The formless Brahman is the breath and the space within the self. . . . There is nothing higher than this, for it is 'the Real of the real'. Living creatures are real and this is their reality.[5]

These two terms, Ātman and Brahman, are used in subtle ways, both distinctly and identically. The ancient gods themselves were thinned down from their thousands into one, and that was Brahman. The only duality that remained was between universal and individual souls and these almost inevitably became identified, so that Brahman and Ātman are often interchangeable terms.

The whole universe is Brahman, and one should calmly worship That as the being in which we live and move and dissolve. . . . It contains all the world; it never speaks and has no care. . . . This Soul of mine in the heart is Brahman, and when I go from here I shall merge into it.[6]

---

[3] Taittirīya Upanishad, 3, 10.6.   [4] Brihad-āranyaka Upanishad, 2.4.
[5] Ibid., 2.3.   [6] Chāndogya Upanishad, 3.14.

Mystical unity in the monistic sense is asserted in 'great words' or utterances, such as 'I am Brahman', and especially 'Thou art That'. This phrase occurred in a series of parables where a philosopher, Uddālaka, instructed his son in the true nature of being. Rejecting the formal priestly education that the boy had received, the father expounded that teaching 'whereby what has not been heard or thought or understood becomes heard, thought and understood'. In nine examples he affirmed that all creatures have Being as their origin, support and dwelling.

That subtle essence is the Soul of the whole universe. That is reality. That is the Soul. You are That.[7]

Bees collect the juices from different trees and reduce them to unity so that they cannot distinguish whether they are the juice of this tree or that. So when creatures merge into Being, they do not know what individuals they were formerly. Similarly, when rivers flow into the sea they do not know their former individuality, but they become that Being.

This unity, indeed identity, of the soul and divine Being, was called *a-dvaita*, non-duality, not-twoness. Western scholars have termed it monism, meaning that there is only one truly existent being. It might be the Pan-en-henism which affirms simple oneness, but some scholars have termed it Pantheism because there is an assumption of a divine being, a transcendent and immanent spirit which seems to be different from merely natural monism.

The Upanishads are fond of analysing the human condition, in a search for the ultimate element, and they often consider the nature of sleep. Dreaming reveals that the soul is a creator who builds his own roads and chariots and bridges. Dreamless sleep is more unified, but in that state the soul has no self-knowledge and appears to be almost destroyed. Therefore there is a final state, beyond dreaming and dreamless sleep. For the most monistic of the Upanishads the soul is not conscious of within or without, it is neither wise nor unwise, it has no distinguishing marks or duality, and this is the fourth state beyond dreamless sleep.[8]

The conclusion from such monistic statements seems to be one of

[7] Ibid., 6.8–16.   [8] Māndūkya Upanishad, 7.

mystical unity but without any characteristics. If the soul is the absolute One, so that it can say 'I am Brahman', then all is the same. There are no differences of individuals or spirits, human or divine, or even of good and evil. We are often told that the perfected soul has passed beyond good and evil and is utterly impassive. This is true world-denial, which is called salvation or rather liberation from the delusion of separateness. It is a mysticism of union and identity, but not of love since love implies some distinction even in union.

The Upanishads are not entirely monistic and a later classical Upanishad speaks of the God who 'stands opposite creatures', the Creator by whose grace one may see the Lord, the One who is himself without colour but distributes colours to others.

> The One who rules over every source,
> in whom the world coheres and dissolves,
> the Lord, giver of blessings, adorable God—
> by revering him one goes to peace forever.[9]

This is a theism, though it stresses also the immanence of the divine being, and it forms a bridge to the theism of the Bhagavad Gītā, which will be considered later. Interpreters of the Upanishads have differed, even over such great utterances as 'You are That'. For some this is fully non-dualistic, but others have interpreted it as a 'qualified non-dualism', since the terms 'you' and 'that' are in apposition. Others attempted to give dualistic or theistic interpretations to these words.

ŚANKARA'S MONISM

The most famous exponent of non-dualism was Śankara, in the eighth century A.D., and he has been called a 'mystic of the soul' since the right knowledge of the soul was his dominant theme. Although he is fundamentally monistic, he spoke in theistic terms at times as a concession to popular needs.

Śankara's mysticism is cool and unimpassioned, and there is argument and assertion rather than autobiography. His goal is the stilling of all activity of will and an abandonment of good and evil

[9] Śvetāśvatara Upanishad, 4.11.

works. This appears in his commentaries on the Upanishads, and especially on the Brahma Sūtra. This work consists of 555 short and enigmatic sentences, of which the first two read:

Therefore inquiry into Brahman.
From which origin of this.

Śankara plunges into his commentary, writing six pages (in the English translation) on the first line, and revealing at once his concept of the identity of the neuter divine being, Brahman, with the soul or self (*ātman*) of everyone:

The existence of Brahman is known on the ground of its being the Self of everyone. For everyone is conscious of the existence of (his) Self, and never thinks 'I am not'. .... And this Self (of whose existence all are conscious) is Brahman.[10]

The proof of the existence of the divine being is in the human self, and this is established by asserting the identity of divine and self. This dogmatic declaration results from reflection and intuition, but it is strongly supported by appeals to the authority of scripture, the Vedas and Upanishads. In this Śankara reveals himself as a theologian rather than a logical philosopher.

He considers passages from the revealed Upanishads in turn, fitting them into his philosophy of monism, so that he is the most thoroughgoing exponent of non-duality, *a-dvaita*. For him the individual and universal souls are not merely united but are fundamentally identical, and this is made quite plain.

If the knowledge of the identity of the Self and Brahman were understood in the way of combination and the like, violence would be done thereby to the connection of the words whose object, in certain passages, it clearly is to intimate the fact of Brahman and the Self being really identical; so, for instance, in the following passages, 'Thou art That', 'I am Brahman', 'This Self is Brahman'.[11]

[10] *The Vedānta-Sūtras with the Commentary by Śankarācārya*, tr. G. Thibaut, 1904, p. 14.
[11] Ibid., p. 31.

Śankara expounded this monism in other writings but he is less happy and faithful when dealing with a more theistic work than the Upanishads, the Bhagavad Gītā. The Gītā contains lines that suit a monistic interpretation, but its main emphasis is theistic and monotheistic. The Gītā speaks of the 'divine birth' of the personal God and his coming to being through Nature by his own power on earth. But Śankara comments that the Lord 'appears to be born and embodied' but 'not in reality, unlike others', and frankly his birth is 'an illusion'.[12]

Even more striking is Śankara's treatment, or lack of it, of the most tremendous chapter in the Gītā. This is the vision of the Universal Form, where the divine being is transfigured in a terrifying and fascinating manner that has no equal in all other religious literature. If ever there was a mystic vision, this is it. But Śankara gives only brief and formal comments, where he does not twist the verses to suit his own monism. This terrifying deity, he says, is indeed the Supreme Being, but 'he is thyself and none else'.

Śankara's teaching is monistic and his mysticism is an impersonal identification of the self and the divine, a realization of the divinity of the soul. Yet he made provision for popular devotion which implied some kind of theism and wrote hymns, an uncommon occupation for a philosopher; although Thomas Aquinas was both philosopher and hymn-writer there have been few modern philosophers who have engaged in hymnody. One of these hymns is addressed to Krishna under the name of Govinda, the cow-herd.

> Chant religious songs more than a thousand times,
> think always of the form of Vishnu . . .
> Worship Govinda, worship Govinda,
> worship Govinda, deluded man.[13]

Yet hymns are only for the spiritually immature, and repetition of the constant refrain might be used for inducing self-hypnosis, in the manner of repetition of the divine name on prayer beads, a practice

---

[12] Bhagavad Gītā, 4.6–9: *The Bhagavad-Gītā with the Commentary of Śrī Śankaracārya*, tr. A. M. Śāstri, 1897, pp. 121 f., 293.

[13] Tr. R. C. Zaehner in *Mysticism Sacred and Profane*, pp. 177 f.

which was later taken from India to Europe. Despite his hymns
Śankara remained a monist; the Brahman of which he wrote in
philosophical works is so characterless as to be not unlike the 'void'
of Buddhist philosophers, and both ancient and modern critics have
called Śankara a 'secret Buddhist'.

ŚANKARA AND ECKHART

One of the most important comparisons of Eastern and Western
mysticism was made some fifty years ago by Rudolf Otto in his
*Mysticism East and West, A Comparative Analysis of the Nature of
Mysticism*. Perhaps to make things difficult for himself, Otto selected
for comparison two men who, despite his claim that they are the
greatest representatives, would be considered by some people as
aberrant: the Indian philosopher Śankara and the Christian
theologian Meister Eckhart.

Eckhart is claimed with wearisome repetition as the great example
of Christian mysticism, usually by those who are not Christian,
because of his apparent monism and self-deification. That twenty-
eight of Eckhart's sentences were condemned by the Avignon Pope
John XXII as heretical did not destroy his influence, but it did mean
that much of his work was lost or badly preserved. Other Christian
mystics have been accused of heresy but it does seem, from what
survives of his teachings, that Eckhart tried to shock his hearers by
speaking of the divine Nothingness, or passing beyond God into the
divine Abyss. Yet even when writing of union with God, Eckhart
held that God is unfathomable and therefore the deification of man
can never reach its end.

In his discussion Otto distinguished two types of mysticism which
were not, as might have been expected, those of East and West or of
monism and theism. Otto claimed that his two types appear in both
East and West, and they are sometimes separate though often linked
together. Both of these types are mystical, but Otto called one 'the
mysticism of *introspection*', and the other 'the mysticism of *unifying
vision*'. The Mysticism of Introspection turns inward, it withdraws
from all outward things, retreats into its own soul, and in the inmost
depths expects to find the Infinite, or God, or Brahman. The world is

not necessary, for only God and the soul are real, and for Śankara even this dualism is dissolved in the one being of the absolute Brahman, for 'You are That'.

Otto's second form of mysticism is the Way of Unity, the unifying vision. Though often confused with the first, it is its direct antithesis, for it knows nothing of inwardness but looks outwards to the world of things and seeks unity under multiplicity. For this unity neither God nor man, neither being nor soul, is necessary in seeking the unity of totality. However, Otto affirms that although these two types of mysticism were originally separate they become closely associated. In particular, in Eckhart and Śankara both these forms of mysticism are found and interpenetrate deeply.

More significant than the suggestion of these two types of mysticism are the similarities and differences which Otto finds between Śankara and Eckhart. They were both opposed to the more popular forms of what might be called mysticism: miraculous activities, occult phenomena and illuminism of any kind. Neither of them claimed to have seen visions or to have had supernatural powers. It might be said, as it was of Wordsworth, and more truly of them, that 'there is no trace of an actual experience' in these intellectualist writers. But this point need not be pressed since later on it will be suggested that mysticism is far wider than either visions or philosophical theories, and that it enters into the experience of most men at many times. Both Śankara and Eckhart were personally averse to emotionalism and they sought union with the divine reality through knowledge, based upon an understanding of real being. They were not nature mystics and they pursued a spiritual or an intellectual path, different from a natural or aesthetic way.

Otto seeks to differentiate between the mysticism of Śankara and that of Eckhart by maintaining that there was a fundamental difference in their religious viewpoints. The determining factor, he says, is the difference in the conception of and relationship to the deity.

The point of departure and the essential distinction is not that the mystic has another and a new relationship to God, but that he has a different God. This difference of object results in a difference of relationship, but it is the difference of the object itself which is the determining factor.[14]

Despite resemblances Śankara and Eckhart are basically different. For Eckhart the union of man with God comes about by divine grace, for Śankara it is by realization of the true nature of the self. Śankara is other-worldly and therefore has no ethic, he is not immoral but a-moral; for Eckhart righteous living comes from obedience to God, and essential righteousness comes from union with the divine essence.

VEDĀNTA AND THE WORLD

The monistic Vedāntic teaching of Śankara has had many followers, though some other commentators on the Vedānta, such as Rāmānuja, strongly differed from monistic teaching. In modern times one of the most notable exponents of non-dualism was the nineteenth-century saint Rāmakrishna and even more his followers. It has been said that Rāmakrishna was torn between his formal Vedāntic teaching and his personal devotion to the Mother (Kālī), yet his modern disciples appear to be much more consistently non-dualistic and less devotional. But there are curious anomalies in the development of this movement.

It has been suggested that Śankara was other-worldly and a-moral, and this seems to follow inevitably from his concern with the only real Ātman-Brahman. Similarly, Rāmakrishna, both in his philosophy and his life of devotion, seems to have cared very little for the world and its needs. On one occasion he was asked about the value of medical work and he replied:

Hospitals, dispensaries, and all such things are unreal. God alone is real. . . . Why should we forget him and destroy ourselves in too many activities? After realizing him, one may, through his grace, become his instruments in building many hospitals and dispensaries.[15]

[14] R. Otto, *Mysticism East and West*. E.T. 1932, Meridian Books edn 1957, pp. 39 f., 140, 207 f.
[15] *The Gospel of Sri Rāmakrishna*, 1942 edn, p. 453.

This might be regarded as continuing traditional monistic teaching and showing an ascetic attitude towards the passing things of life, which were illusory anyway. But Rāmakrishna seems to have been more pantheistic or even theistic than monistic. He spoke of being quickened by 'the Lord's grace', and liking 'no other words than those relating to God'. He claimed that by perfect knowledge one could see God in everything and in all kinds of men. 'I see that it is he who is moving about in different forms, now as an honest man, now as a cheat and again as a villain.' Even lust and anger in man are passions which come from God; they cannot be eradicated but they can be educated and turned into passion for God. This is very different from the a-moral and passionless detachment of Śankara.

The Rāmakrishna Mission (significant term) introduced social elements at an early period. First of all it was teaching that was recommended, for all castes, with disinterested holy men going from village to village teaching education and better ways of life. The objects of the Mission were defined in a Memorandum of 1909 as, among others, 'to establish, maintain, carry on and assist schools, colleges, orphanages, workshops, laboratories, hospitals, dispensaries, houses for the infirm, the invalid and the afflicted, famine-relief works, and other educational and charitable works and institutions of a like nature'. This wide range of social activity may have owed something, perhaps much, to the example of Christian missions. All that needs to be noted here is that such activities were not regarded by the leaders of the movement as incompatible with mystical and non-dualistic philosophy.

Chapter 5

INTEGRATION AND ISOLATION: YOGA AND JAIN

EARLY YOGA

Parallel with monism and theism in India, though often closely related to one or the other, there are forms of mystical belief and practice, such as Yoga and Jainism, which seem to have neither the Absolute nor God for inspiration. The varieties of Yoga are often thought to be outstanding examples of Indian mysticism, but if this is so they tend to be mysticisms of the soul rather than of God, since they concentrate upon the soul. Or rather it is the plurality of souls which are considered, since they exist in infinite number, and similar beliefs are found in the religion of Jainism.

On a few seals found in the remains of the Indus civilization, from before 1500 B.C., there is a figure seated cross-legged like a Yogi, wearing a horned headdress, with perhaps three faces and surrounded by jungle animals. Since all these features can be paralleled in later descriptions of the god Śiva, who is often called Lord of Yoga, this figure has been called a proto-Śiva or a Proto-Yogi. As this pre-dates the Vedas, which do not mention Yoga, it has been thought that Yoga and related teachings, including Jainism and perhaps Buddhism, go back to a remote and non-Aryan antiquity which knows nothing of the monistic philosophy of the later Vedas and Upanishads. Whether the Proto-Yogi of the Indus seals is a god or a man, he may be turned in upon himself to seek that integration of the soul which is Yogic mysticism.

When Yogic terminology appears in the later Upanishads it means

43

both the yoking or disciplining of the senses and the yoking or joining of the individual with the great Self or Supreme Spirit.

> Through the Yoga-study of what belongs to the self the wise man perceives the ancient dweller in the hidden depths, considers him as God, and leaves joy and sorrow.[1]

Later Yoga practice is prescribed, in a quiet level spot near to water where one should hold the body steady, check movements, control breathing and calm the mind. There may be delusions of lights and smoke in early stages, but health and steadiness should be the result. The aim is to 'become unitary' and 'by knowing God' to be 'freed from all chains'.[2]

The Bhagavad Gītā gives a similar description of the bodily and mental discipline of Yogic meditation, but it is even more insistent that the goal of meditation is God, rather than self or a void. Control of mind and integration of personality are practices of Yoga but the goal is to be rapt in God and to find the calm of Nirvāna which exists in him.

> With tranquil soul and free from fear
> abide in vows of chastity,
> with thoughts on me, controlled in mind
> and integrated, rapt in me.[3]

The Gītā is claimed as the Gospel of Yoga and editors have named each of its eighteen chapters after the Yoga of that particular teaching. Its use of the word Yoga shows many shifts of meaning, and there are yogas of knowledge, works, devotion, meditation and so on, but the culmination of the Gītā is in a union with God which is mystical theism.

Very different from this Upanishadic and Gītā theism are the teachings of the traditional Sāmkhya and Yoga philosophy. Sāmkhya 'enumeration' (or 'calculation' or 'distinctionism') distinguishes the basic principles of Nature and Spirit. Nature (*Prakriti*) is first at rest in timeless quiescence, then it evolves the

---

[1] Katha Upanishad, 2.12.
[2] Śvetāśvatara Upanishad, 2.8–15.
[3] Bhagavad Gītā, 6.14.

universe from itself, which after the cycle of ages is dissolved and reabsorbed into Nature. This might seem to be like a nature mysticism of identification with nature or the one. But this would ignore the essential, though isolated, place of Spirit in the Sāmkhya system. For Spirit (*Purusha*), or rather countless spirits, forms a collection of individual monads, or eternal beings, which have no communication with each other. The souls are attracted to Nature when it begins to evolve, and they are related to psycho-physical bodies for a time, though essentially they are unattached. And Nature, when it has ceased to evolve and to manifest itself to Spirit, returns to quiescence.

> As a dancer ceases dancing
> when she has shown herself on the stage,
> so Nature ceases producing
> when she has shown herself to Spirit . . .
> Nothing is more modest than Nature,
> which says, I have been seen,
> and shows herself no more to Spirit.[4]

Although the relationship of Spirit and Nature in Sāmkhya teaching may have been something like a sexual union, comparable to the Chinese Yang and Yin, whereby the universe came into being and by whose harmony it is sustained, yet Sāmkhya developed away from this notion. From a mysticism of union with Nature, the goal is to deliver souls from her loving embrace and lead them to isolation. The three constituent Strands or Qualities of Nature, which are goodness, passion and darkness, bind the embodied soul by attaching it to knowledge, pleasure or sloth. The aim of yogic discipline is liberation from these strands, into the peace of detachment. The male Spirit, freed from female Nature, passes beyond nature mysticism into the passionless isolation of the countless monads. The goal is both integration of oneself and isolation from all others.

When Yoga teaching came to join with Sāmkhya philosophy it was defined as 'restraint of the fluctuations of the mind' in the famous and probably pre-Christian Yoga Sūtras of Patañjali. Such restraint

---

[4] Sāmkhya Kārikā, 59–61.

would make the seer 'abide in himself' in an isolation of the soul and a superior concentration. Later the eight limbs or parts of Yoga are given as restraint, observance, posture, breath-control, sense-withdrawal, concentration, meditation and contemplation. All of these lead to self-control, integration and self-union.

But then another way of concentration is suggested which appears to be less self-contained if not theistic:

> Or it [concentration] may be attained by devotion to the Lord, who is a special kind of Spirit untouched by affliction, works, results or impressions. . . . The word that expresses him is the mystical syllable [OM], and it should be repeated, with reflection on its meaning.[5]

With such words this soul-mysticism seems to move to a form of God-mysticism, introducing a Lord as object of devotion and means of concentration. But this Lord (*īśvara*) is not God, in the full sense. He is one Spirit (*purusha*) among many, perhaps more than first among equals yet merely an alternative aid to meditation. This Spirit was untouched by involvement with Nature, and the purpose of concentration upon him is only temporary. It is not to enter into abiding union with God (as in the Gītā), but rather to break free from the embraces of Nature. It may be that some Yogis needed an object of devotion, seeking for God, but what is provided here is a divinity subservient to the overriding aim of breaking away from entanglement with the body, into a truly other-worldly solitude. This may be a soul-mysticism but it is not a God-mysticism, even if a move has been made in that direction and even if functionally the object of devotion might be more important than in theory.

The Lord, admitted by Patañjali in his Yoga Sūtras, perhaps third century B.C., is available to Yogis who have already chosen the path of discipline for self-purification and he plays only a small part in the standard texts. But in later Yoga commentators he plays a larger role and becomes a God who by his will makes men do good deeds or makes others commit evil deeds. God draws men 'like a magnet' and his 'special mercy' seems to reflect the theism of the Gītā. It was a tribute to the strength of mystical and devotional

[5] Yoga Sūtras, 1.23–8.

movements of later times that teachers of Yoga gave such importance to the Lord.

LATER YOGA

The classical texts of Yoga indicate supernormal powers that Yogis may attain, but for them spiritual advancement, calm and integration are the real aims of Yoga and bring man to the true goal of spiritual freedom. No doubt at that time, and many times later, there have been practitioners of Yoga who have emphasized the magical and miraculous powers which they claim to have gained: levitation, walking through fire, burial alive, becoming invisible, flying through the air, and the like. Hatha Yoga, the Yoga of 'violent exercise', more seriously concentrates upon difficult and sometimes dangerous postures for physical and mental discipline, but a modern practitioner declared at the end of his course that there was 'nothing supernatural' and had been 'no miracles'. Other varieties emphasize different practices; Mantra-Yoga, with texts or spells, teaches repetition of words or syllables in order to achieve abstraction of consciousness or supernormal states; Laya-Yoga, Yoga of Dissolution, seeks to arouse and develop latent bodily powers beyond normal capacity. The central body of teaching and practice is the Rāja Yoga, the Royal Yoga taught by Patañjali.

Modern teachers of Yoga often introduce into their expositions what is called 'the god of one's choice' (*ishta-devatā*). This term would be shocking to a true monotheist, especially non-Hindu, but it follows the suggestion of the Yoga Sūtras that a Lord may be used for one's own purification, and in such a context mystical union would not be with the Lord but with oneself. On a monist view of an absolute Brahman, methods of Yoga may also include use of a Lord in the lower stages of devotion but this would be superseded in the final non-duality.

By contrast a modern teaching of Integral Yoga, inaugurated by Aurobindo Ghose (1872–1950, philosopher and founder of a spiritual centre at Pondicherry, South India) criticizes non-dualism and is more truly theistic. Advaita Vedānta, it is said, teaches Being-Consciousness-Bliss but then gets rid of the last two and throws everything back on to the first and most abstract 'pure featureless existence'. This is 'Buddhistic philosophy' and it is abstracted to 'an infinite zero'. Aurobindo, on the contrary, taught neither separate existence nor non-existence but 'the conscious Being' of God, and such a faith brings union with God on earth and beyond.

> Our aim is . . . to live in the Divine, the Infinite, in God, and not in any mere egoism and temporality, but at the same time not apart from Nature, from our fellow beings, from earth and mundane existence, any more than the Divine lives aloof from us and the world.[6]

Aurobindo had a non-Hindu education, trained in Christian schools in India and England, and coming to Sanskrit studies only after learning Latin and Greek. Yet from his return to India he became immersed in Hindu theology and philosophy and his extensive writings have few overt references to European and Christian works, though their influence may be present. In pursuit of his theistic teaching he proposed Integral Yoga to bring together body and soul, individual and community, and all activities. Its aim was:

> A sound individual and social body and the satisfaction of the legitimate needs and demands of the material mind, sufficient ease, leisure, equal opportunity, so that the whole of mankind, and no longer only the favoured race, class or individual may be free to develop the emotional and intellectual being to its full capacity.

The 'Life Divine' demands:

> The realisation by the individual that only in the life of his fellowmen is his own life complete. There must be the realisation by the race that only on the free and full life of the individual can its own perfection and permanent happiness be founded.[7]

The Aurobindo Ashram at Pondicherry demonstrates this Integral Yoga wherein the whole of life, spiritual, educational, industrial and agricultural, should practise the principles of the

[6] *The Synthesis of Yoga*, 1948, pp. 660, 497.
[7] Aurobindo, *The Ideal of Human Unity*, 1919, p. 21.

founder, and the new city of Auroville is planned to demonstrate the divine life of supermen. Yet it is strange that the monistic Rāmakrishna Mission is much more widespread than the theistic Aurobindo movement. There may be personal and social reasons for this, but the Rāmakrishna Mission is found throughout India and in other continents, and it is associated with a wide range of social concerns.

Although, or because, Yoga is very ancient in India it has been valued and adopted by nearly all other religious movements. Not only did Yoga enter into theistic and monistic religions within Hinduism, but it also profoundly influenced other religions, such as Jainism and Buddhism. An eminent authority states that 'in the universal history of mysticism, classic Yoga occupies a place of its own, and one that is difficult to define'. It reacted against, or was different from, the theisms of Hinduism, and it sought 'to realize absolute concentration in order to attain enstasis', yet it entered into both theistic and non-theistic religions.[8] The yoking of Yoga is primarily a discipline which seeks the integration of self and its isolation in bliss, in a soul-mysticism or self-union, but it has often been adapted to the other major meaning of Yoga, a yoking in union in a God-mysticism.

JAIN ISOLATION

Sāmkhya and Yoga may have developed principles already present in Jainism, which is claimed by its adherents as a very ancient Indian religion, and which may represent some religion of the Indus Valley period or even earlier, non-Aryan or non-Vedic. Jainism and Buddhism are reckoned as heterodox because they teach doctrines outside the Brahminic orthodoxy of the Vedānta. The Jains are few in numbers today, but they survived down the ages when Buddhism had virtually disappeared from India, though Buddhism differed from Jainism in being a successful missionary religion over much of the rest of Asia. Like the Buddhists, the Jains do not believe in an eternal creator God, though some of the Hindu gods and their own Jinas, the 'victorious', are prominent in Jain buildings and worship.

[8] M. Eliade, *Yoga, Immortality and Freedom*. E.T. 1958, p. 361.

But while Buddhists deny or are agnostic about the soul, it is central to Jain teaching. If they have a mysticism it will be a soul-mysticism as in much of Yoga.

For the Jains the universe is eternal, passing through infinite cosmic cycles of emergence, florescence and dissolution. In each cycle there appear Jinas or Tīrthankaras, 'fordmakers', who not only themselves cross the river of transmigration but teach the way of salvation to others. In the present world aeon there have appeared twenty-four Tīrthankaras, of whom the first lived millions of years ago and the last, Mahāvīra, 'great hero', was an older contemporary of Gautama the Buddha.

In Jain doctrine the soul (*jīva*, comparable to the Hindu *ātman*) is eternal yet acquires many different forms. There are countless souls, not only in human beings and animals but in plants, rocks and the elements of lights and winds.

> The essence of the soul is life, the capacity of being liberated. . . .
> There are worldly and liberated souls, with mind and without mind, mobile and immobile. . . . Those with minds are knowers.[9]

The whole universe is alive but souls are imprisoned by matter, the result of Karma, and liberation can come only when all the layers of Karma, good and bad, are dissolved. The famous Jain doctrine of non-violence (*a-himsā*, not hurting) derives both from belief in animal souls and also from the need for purification from violent deeds.

Jains, like Hindus and Buddhists, believe in the round of transmigration and reincarnation, into pleasant or evil births according to Karma previously acquired. It seems that many souls will reincarnate indefinitely as the universe passes through endless cycles. Not only monks but laymen are expected to undergo strict discipline, vegetarianism, fasting and penance, to attain a better rebirth if not Nirvāna. The householder is enjoined to 'limit his activity to a fixed place', feed guests and saints, have compassion for all living beings, and 'contemplate the soul'.[10]

The goal of Jain discipline is Nirvāna and the nature of this

[9] Tattvārthādhigama Sūtra of Umāsvāti, tr. J. L. Jaini, 1920, ch. 2.
[10] Ibid., 7.

state differs from monistic Hindu or agnostic Buddhist ideas because of the concept of the soul, which is more akin to Yoga ideas. The Jains attacked the monistic doctrine of the identity of individual and universal soul as vigorously as they criticized Mahāyāna Buddhist identification of transmigration and Nirvāna.

> If the soul was only one, there would be no happiness or sorrow, bondage or liberation. If the soul was all-pervading, there would be no bondage or liberation.
>
> But that there are many souls, like many pots and other worldly things, is proved from their different characteristics.[11]

The soul is eternal and indestructible, but it is bound by karmic matter from which it must be freed to rise to Nirvāna. There is no Supreme Being to help in this struggle and the other gods are themselves caught in the round of transmigration, while the liberated Jinas are free from all concern with the world. The soul, by discipline and knowledge, frees itself and rises through the spheres of the universe, changing colour as it goes from dark to light. Jain texts compare its progress to a bubble rising to the surface of water, or to a gourd whose clay covering melts away in water so that it bobs up to the surface. Thus the soul, rid of karmic matter, rises from the imprisonment of the world up to the ceiling of the universe. Beyond the gods and all currents of transmigration, the soul abides forever in solitary bliss in Nirvāna.

Nirvāna is at the summit of all, where disembodied souls dwell in endless calm. Other Jinas and Tirthankaras ('ford-makers') are there but each soul dwells in 'isolation' (*kevala* or *kaivalya*), a notion that is found also in the Yoga Sūtras of Patañjali. The state of mystical purity is a self-unity, integration and isolation. The Buddhist Nirvāna is not dissimilar despite its negative view of the soul, and Hindu monism with its identification of Brahman and ātman is comparable at least in this that there is a self-union rather than a Beatific Vision of the Deity as in theistic mysticism.

In theory Nirvāna is attainable in this world and the lives of the Jinas give standard descriptions of such attainment. It is said of Mahāvira:

[11] Ganadharavāda of Jinabhadra, 1.32–9.

He reached Nirvāna, the complete and full, the unobstructed, unimpeded, infinite and supreme, the best knowledge and intuition called Kevala. . . . Omniscient and comprehending all objects, he knew all conditions of the world, of gods, men and demons.

Yet Mahāvira, like the Buddha, after attaining Nirvāna did not at once leave the world for the ceiling of the universe, and it seems that compassion got the better of isolation, since he taught his doctrine to the world:

When the venerable ascetic Mahāvira had reached the highest knowledge and intuition, he reflected on himself and the world; first he taught the law to the gods and afterwards to men.[12]

Jain mysticism of unification and isolation seems restricted and abstract and its non-theistic doctrines might appear to leave little room for warmer or more popular devotion, and yet the strong human desire for objects of worship finds outlets in Jain art and ritual. The twenty-four Jinas are represented in statues in Jain temples, which are places of worship and sacrificial offering. Mahāvira, in particular, appears in paintings and sculptures, while in literature his life serves as a model for those of more legendary Jinas and the stories reflect the ideals and aspirations of worshippers.

The subject of prayer in Jainism is delicate, since there is no eternal creator and the lesser gods are transmigrating and must be reborn as men before attaining Nirvāna. But it is admitted that laymen do pray to Hindu gods and some of them, notably Lakshmi, the consort of Vishnu, are very popular. The images of the Jinas in temples are justified as models of virtue and calm. Contemplating the image of a Jina should fill the mind with a need for renunciation, purify it, and prepare it for Nirvāna.

At home the pious Jain rises before dawn and, with rosary of 108 beads in hand, salutes the five classes of embodied and disembodied great beings, all the holy ones in the world and beyond.

The Jinas who have attained Nirvānic isolation at the top of the universe are said to be beyond all care and unaffected by the troubles of the world with its inhabitants. But there are texts which show that

---

[12] Āchārānga Sūtra, 2.15.

human need attributed continuing interest and communion to the Jinas.

> May the blessed give great joy, protect you, release you, destroy your misfortunes. . . . May there be good fortune from Mahāvīra's eyes, whose pupils are wide with compassion even for sinful people, moist with a trace of tears.[13]

[13] Quoted in my *Avatar and Incarnation*, 1970, p. 189; see also my *Worship in the World's Religions*, 1961 and 1974, pp. 66 f.

Chapter 6

BUDDHA AND NIRVĀNA

IS IT MYSTICAL?

The place of Buddhism among the religions has often been debated and definitions of religion have been enlarged to include those systems which appear to have no deity yet clearly have a long and powerful religious culture. Early Buddhism at least seemed not only to be agnostic about God, like the Jains, but also about the soul, and some have therefore maintained that Buddhism began as a philosophy or ethic and degenerated into a religion. Others, however, maintain that Buddhism was religious from the outset and much richer than critical study might assume.

In the nineteenth century, rationalistic colonial administrators, or armchair students in the West, often imagined Buddhism to be a godless and soulless utilitarian system, but two recent anthropological studies of Ceylon and Burma claim that Buddhist practice is often different from theory. Melford Spiro thought that traditional Buddhism would present a challenge to some of the traditional notions about the nature of man and religion, but when he arrived in Burma the problem 'turned out to be a pseudo-problem'. First, because some of the notions held about Buddhism are not characteristic of it, and secondly, because other doctrines are rejected or ignored by the faithful. So that 'Studies of living Buddhism have shown that Buddhists differ very little from people in general.'[1] People believe in Buddhas and gods, worship them and

[1] M. Spiro, *Buddhism and Society*, 1971, pp. 10 f.; see also R. F. Gombrich, *Precept and Practice*, 1971.

pray to them, speak of their souls and hope for personal rebirth, meditate little and regard Nirvāna as a far distant goal.

As far as mysticism goes the great Japanese scholar D. T. Suzuki stated, 'I grow firmly convinced that the Christian experiences are not after all different from those of the Buddhist.' But it is not surprising that Suzuki in his study of mysticism spent much of his time comparing Buddhism with the teachings of Meister Eckhart. Further, he was expounding the northern Mahayānā Buddhism, which has great richness and variety in its expressions of the supernatural.[2]

The doctrines and texts of traditional southern Theravāda (Hīnayāna) Buddhism, however, appear to pose a problem for mysticism, if it seeks any kind of unity. If philosophically-minded monks rejected the idea of the soul, along with God, then both God-mysticism and soul-mysticism seem to disappear, making a great exception on the Indian scene and among world religions, showing original Buddhism to be unmystical. It might be argued that if the mystic is seeking unity, whether in his self or in the absolute Brahman, what he is seeking is not his self but the unity, though how unity could be conceived without either subject or object is not easy to say. However, the early texts are more complex than this might suggest.

Of Gautama the Buddha himself many stories are told in the canonical scriptures about experiences which might be described as mystical. The Buddha-to-be practised different forms of Yoga and asceticism, before rejecting them in favour of his Middle Way between the extremes of sensuality and austerity. Both at his enlightenment and death the Buddha attained to a unifying vision and passed through trance states before the final peace of Nirvāna. He 'attained and abode in the first trance of joy and pleasure', and passed on to the second, third and fourth trances, which gave knowledge of his former existences, the vision of beings being born and reborn, knowledge of Four Noble Truths, and the destruction of desires.

As I knew and perceived this, my mind was freed from desires of the senses, from desire for existence, and from ignorance. As I was

[2] D. T. Suzuki, *Mysticism Christian and Buddhist*, 1957, p. 8.

liberated knowledge arose that I was liberated. I understood that rebirth was destroyed, that the religious life had been led, that what had to be done was done, and that there was no more for me in this world.[3]

This is claimed as a series of trances, and there seems to have been self-unity but no divine union. Gautama himself, as far as one can tell from the discourses attributed to him, did not believe in a Supreme Being. But these discourses seem to have been put into their present form centuries after his death and, while they may contain some of his thoughts, much else must be the later reflection of his followers. There are references to a creator deity, Brahmā, but he is simply the first to emerge from chaos at the beginning of each world aeon, and as the first he claims to be supreme.

The Upanishadic Brahman, as an absolute Being in union with the soul, was apparently not considered by the Buddha. But early Buddhist texts do speak of 'becoming Brahman' in the sense of liberation into Nirvāna. It is often said that the goal is to be 'without desire, cool, having joy, and oneself become Brahman'. The Buddha himself is said to have 'become all sight, become all wisdom, become the truth (dhamma), become Brahman'.[4] This is the state of those who have gained enlightenment and found their home in Nirvāna.

While Hindu thinkers were concerned with the eternal being of Brahman and its relationship with the process of becoming, absolute existence and the material world, Buddhism sought salvation from the world into the timeless state. In his famous first sermon the Buddha analysed the human condition in the Noble Truth of Pain: birth is painful, so are age, illness, death, sorrow, mourning, dejection and despair. The Noble Truth of the Cause of Pain is craving or desire: craving for pleasure and passion, craving for existence or non-existence. The Noble Truth of the Cessation of Pain is the cessation of craving which means abandoning it, forsaking it, releasing it, non-attachment to it. And the Noble Truth of the Way which leads to the cessation of pain is the Noble Eightfold Way of mental and moral discipline: right views, resolve, speech, action,

[3] Mahā-Saccaka Sutta, 1.242.
[4] Dīgha Nikāya, 3.233; Samyutta Nikāya, 4.94–5.

livelihood, effort, mindfulness and concentration. This is not unlike the eight limbs of Yoga which led to integration and isolation.

NIRVĀNA

The goal of Buddhist discipline is that Nirvāna which has been described as 'become Brahman'. But it is not a union of the soul with the divine, or even with the abstract, since the nature and existence of the soul is a much-debated problem. That there is no permanent ego or self is maintained in the Buddhist doctrine of not-self or non-soul (*anattā*), which is taught in the Buddha's second sermon and must therefore be a cardinal subject. The body is not-self, for if it were it could not be subject to illness. Similarly the feelings, perceptions, habits and consciousness are considered in turn to show that they are not the soul. There is no personal survival of death, because we are bundles of different qualities which are dissolved at death. The aim of action is not to deny or suppress the ego but to realize that it does not really exist.

Whether there is an ethereal or eternal soul is not clear. The soul or self is refused identity with any of the five constituent elements of the personality, but 'nothing is said either way about its existence or non-existence quite apart from them. The Buddha never taught that the self is "not", but only that "it cannot be apprehended".'[5] Buddhists, like Hindus and others, believe in rebirth, though the link between lives is made by Karma, the deeds and their entail which lead to the formation of another psycho-physical organism.

The goal is Nirvāna, a term used by Jains and Buddhists before its adoption into Hinduism. Nirvāna is commonly but wrongly interpreted in the West as extinction in the sense of complete annihilation. But it is extinction of desires, not of all being. Yet there is no personal survival in Nirvāna, since there is no such thing as a person or individuality after the round of births and deaths has been broken by the attainment of the perfectly enlightened state of 'become Brahman'. To be reborn in any form is to remain in the realm of transmigration, whereas in Nirvāna there is no becoming of any kind.

[5] E. Conze, *Buddhist Thought in India*, 1962, p. 39.

Nirvāna means 'blowing out', as the flames of desire are blown out on attaining peace. There is no longer any craving, or sensation, but one is brought to a stillness, or extinguished in phenomenal existence. Popular texts speak more affirmatively of Nirvāna and in the classical *Questions of Milinda* it is said that while Nirvāna cannot be pointed out, and it is not past, present or future, yet there is Nirvāna and it is known by the mind. Nirvāna is compared to a wishing jewel and a mountain peak; it grants all that one can desire, brings joy and sheds light, and is lofty, exalted and infinite. Yet in earlier texts it means the cooling of desire, peace, health, the unborn and undying eternal state and experience.

It is noteworthy that when the Bhagavad Gītā, which appears to have been much influenced by Buddhist teachings in its early chapters, used these terms it made subtle changes in preparation for its own theistic doctrines. The Gītā seems to have been the first Hindu text to have adopted the word Nirvāna and it appears in the Buddhist sense of peace or immortality. But it is joined with Brahman, to make a compound Brahman–Nirvāna, which seems to have been invented by the author of the Gītā, to express a firm, steady state which one may attain on earth and to which one goes at death. This peace which culminates in Nirvāna subsists in God himself, according to the Gītā.[6]

Early Buddhist texts generally speak of Nirvāna in negatives, and therefore some writers have assumed that Buddhism was purely practical and believed in no eternal reality. But a well-known text insists that there is a state of being where there is no earth or water, no world here or hereafter, no coming or going, which does not develop or depend on anything else.

> There is an unborn, unmade, unbecome and incomposite; for if there were not there would be no escape from what is born, made, become or compounded. But a way of escape can be seen from the born, made, become and compounded, because there is an unborn, unmade, unbecome and incomposite.[7]

As in Jainism, the need for objects of worship, and even

[6] Bhagavad Gītā, 2.72; 6.15.
[7] Udāna, p. 80.

communion with them, has powerfully influenced popular Buddhism
from the beginning. If this doctrine taught at first a path of mental
and moral discipline for monks, it is recorded that one of the first
converts to the preaching of the Buddha was a layman: the merchant
Tapussa from Orissa, and his companion Bhallika, uttered the
Twofold, later Threefold, Refuge, the Three Jewels, which has
remained the constant recitation of Theravāda Buddhism ever since:

> I go to the Buddha for refuge,
> I go to the Doctrine (*dhamma*) for refuge,
> I go to the Order (*sangha*) for refuge.

To go for refuge indicates communion; the phrase is used in the
Bhagavad Gītā of going to Krishna for salvation and it appears in a
similar sense in later Buddhist writings. Does this mean that the
Buddha is a god? Not strictly, since the gods are part of the universal
cycle and the Buddha is above it all, but in fact he is called the 'god
above the gods' (*devātideva*) and many attitudes suggest that
functionally he fills the role of object of worship.

According to Theravāda Buddhist theory the Buddha was a man,
the best of all and one who showed the way, but now either he does
not exist at all or in Nirvāna he is as impassive as the Tīrthankaras of
Jainism. He is a signpost pointing the way to salvation rather than an
active Saviour. But practice is often different from theory or, as one
writer puts it, 'Even this cognitive position is not consistently
maintained in the ritual context.'[8]

The canonical accounts of the Buddha's death and cremation
state that his relics were divided among eight regions, each of which
made a cairn over them, and similar *stūpas*, with relics of the Buddha
and his disciples, became popular in Buddhist lands and helped in the
establishment of the faith. The foundation of a Buddhist temple at
Chiswick in 1964 was marked by the arrival of a relic, said to be the
first Buddhist relic in Europe, accompanied by the Prime Minister of
Ceylon, Mrs Bandaranaike. When Buddhists visit shrines or relics
they take offerings of flowers, incense and lights, calling upon the
Buddha as 'Lord of sages', 'Dispeller of darkness', and asking him to
'accept this food from us, taking compassion on us'.

[8] R. Gombrich, *Precept and Practice*, p. 142; and see pp. 115 f., 140.

The Buddha is represented by countless images and these are honoured by offerings and ceremonies. The images are not mere representations or memorials, for there is an 'eye festival', a final ceremony, which gives the image such a powerful gaze, potentially dangerous, that it cannot be borne direct and the craftsman paints in the eyes by looking in a mirror. An early witness declared of the image that 'the Eyes being formed, it is thenceforward a God', and later study confirms this statement. The Buddha is felt to be a living presence and a widely known Pali verse implores him, 'Forgive me my transgression'. Hence even in Theravāda Buddhism there is not only the indescribable state of Nirvāna but a communion with the Buddha.

BUDDHA-NATURE AND BODHISATTVAS

Philosophers of Mahāyāna Buddhism, beginning in northern India and continuing over central and eastern Asia, proceeded to speak of Nirvāna in even more negative terms, though this could tend towards a monistic mysticism. Since one should not grasp after an individual, a self or a being, the Buddha himself has not set beings free because there are no beings to set free. Similarly although countless beings are said to have been led to Nirvāna, in reality no beings at all have entered Nirvāna, since there are no beings to lead there. Indeed there is no transmigration or Nirvāna, or transmigration is Nirvāna, because all conceptions are false. So one arrives at the Void or absolute emptiness.

The doctrine of emptiness spread throughout Mahāyāna, not only in the negative sense of denying a personal self, but in the wider sense of fulfilment. Set free from the limitations of existence and ideas into the vastness of emptiness, philosophers found there an identity with the Buddha-nature. There is a curious parallel, here, as elsewhere, with Islam wherein the unity of God becomes a unity with all beings. Some Mahāyānists regarded the Void as the Buddha-nature and the final Nirvāna, and this must exist in all beings.

A concept of 'sameness' was used to indicate the immanence of the Buddha-nature, the same in all beings. Hence all beings have the Buddha-nature, or are at least potential Buddhas.

BUDDHA AND NIRVĀNA

The road to Buddhahood is open to all.
At all times have all living beings the Germ of
    Buddhahood in them.
If the Element of the Buddha did not exist (in everyone)
There could be no disgust with suffering,
Nor could there be a wish for Nirvāna.[9]

It is the Buddha within us who both makes us long for Nirvāna and sets us free. We can become Buddhas because we already are such potentially. Saints are much the same as ordinary people, though they have the special character of the enlightened. As the English translator comments, this Void and Buddha-nature doctrine of Buddhism is very much like other doctrines of pantheism.

On a practical level some Mahāyāna Buddhist schools, notably Zen, have taught their followers to rely on the 'self-power' of their own efforts, rather than on the 'other-power' of Buddhas and gracious beings in various forms of Mahāyāna. Zen has made a great appeal in the West because of its apparently rational teachings, with less supernaturalism and theology than most religions, and this has seemed to harmonize with Western sceptical and utilitarian ideas. Western converts tend to ignore or disdain the devotional practices which Zen disciples in Asia use regularly even as part of their growth in 'self-power'. There are probably no Zen temples in Asia that do not witness regular offerings before statues of Gautama or Amida, Kwanyin or Manjushri. Reverence to supernatural beings is thought to be natural and right, and even a means to avoid falling into the delusions of egotism.

However, apologists for devotional methods in 'self-power' schools seem to want to have the best of both worlds, profane and theistic. It has been maintained that a Zen meditator on the Void and a theist who feels a divine response have 'an identical experience'. But this is to misunderstand the theistic claim. A believer in God does not make use of him in order to gain a feeling, indeed he cannot do so. He does not seek a response from an unknown or remote

---

[9] Ratnagotravibhaga, 1, 28.40, tr. E. Conze in *Buddhist Texts*, 1954, pp. 168 f. See also E. Conze, *Buddhist Thought in India*, pp. 229 f.

deity, but himself responds to the previous action of a living God. In
biblical terms, 'We love, because he first loved us.'

Those who seek to go 'beyond the gods' show that they do not
really believe in the gods as gods. 'Let God be God', said Luther. So
it is not surprising that these writers, who are apparently not theists,
claim that their doctrines are 'invisible to minds befogged by concepts
such as good and evil'.[10] Gods are interested in human behaviour,
rewarding right and punishing wrong, and so is any Buddha worth
his salt. The man who relies on 'self-power' may too easily be
concerned only with his own isolation or the dissipation of his ego,
and without concern for less fortunate creatures. Hence arises the
criticism that some mystics are anti-social, and seek neither social
reform nor the removal of injustices, since such things are irrelevant
if there are no beings to deliver.

Most of Mahāyāna Buddhism, however, took a different view and
taught a 'great vehicle' (mahā-yāna) whereby all beings would be
saved. Early Buddhism spoke of some Pratyeka Buddhas,
'enlightened singly', who sought Nirvāna for themselves alone, and
lived like lonely rhinoceroses. But the great Mahāyāna scripture, The
Lotus of the True Law, which is as important for northern Buddhism
as the Bhagavad Gītā is for Hinduism, gave new teachings on
Nirvāna, on Buddhas and on service.

The Lotus Sūtra speaks of the 'middling wisdom' and 'middling
enlightenment' of those who are afraid of the world and think they
have escaped from it and reached Nirvāna. But in reality it is only by
knowing the universal laws that Nirvāna is reached, and these are
taught by the Buddha alone, for he is 'the Lord, who has no superior,
who appears in this world to save'.[11] He proclaims the truth to all
creatures, high and low, intelligent and dull. He teaches by one sole
vehicle, the Buddha-vehicle, to bring salvation to all. When he
declared this some of the ascetics retired from him, but most beings
in all the worlds welcomed this universal message.

Like Krishna in the Gītā, and like the uncreated Brahman, the
Buddha in the Lotus Sūtra is called Father of the world, the Self-

[10] J. Blofeld, *Beyond the Gods*, 1974, pp. 18, 160.
[11] Saddharma Pundarīka, 5.78–82; tr. H. Kern, *The Lotus of the True Law*,
1909, pp. 40, 140.

born, the Saviour, the Protector of all creatures. It is true that he seemed to have died on earth and entered Nirvāna, but 'this was a device of mine' since 'you would not obey my words, unless the Lord of the world enter Nirvāna'. But in reality he is endless and timeless, revealing himself to his disciples and saving myriads of beings.[12]

In the favourite twenty-fourth chapter of the Lotus Sūtra, devotion is directed towards the great Bodhisattva Avalokitesvara, the Lord who looks or is looked upon.

> He with his powerful knowledge beholds all creatures who are beset with many hundreds of troubles and afflicted by many sorrows, and thereby is a Saviour in the world, including the gods.[13]

This gracious being saves all creatures who call upon him in any kind of trouble. One only has to think upon him to become like him, since he beholds all beings with compassion and is the perfection of all virtues. As with the Buddha himself, it is prayed that we may 'soon become like thee'. Realization of the Buddha-wisdom comes from union with the Buddha-nature. Such mystical participation in the 'transcendent body' of the Buddha is comparable with the Hindu Rāmānuja's doctrine of selves as the body of the Supreme Being.

A cardinal Mahāyāna doctrine is that of the Bodhi-sattva, the 'enlightenment-being', or one whose 'essence is enlightenment'. This is one who has progressed far on the path and is on the brink of Nirvāna, but then refuses to enter it until all other creatures are saved. This is a doctrine of compassion, in which love has replaced Nirvāna as the ideal, and it has generally been taken as one of the major distinctions between Mahāyāna and Theravāda religion and ethics. There does seem to have been a dilemma here for Theravāda, for if self-restraint and the lonely search for Nirvāna had been consistently pursued there might have been numerous forest ascetics but hardly any popular religion. Today, Gombrich states, 'In fact most people, even monks, say that meditation is impracticable, offering some such excuse as the pressure of affairs or the decline of the doctrine, and they display very little liking for *Nirvāna*.' People

---

[12] Lotus Sūtra, 15.7–21.
[13] Ibid., 24.17.

seek rather for a good rebirth by acts of merit, and these are more likely to be active giving of alms than negative self-restraint.[14] That this is not merely a foreign or modern judgement is shown by the Lotus Sūtra itself in its judgement on the lonely ascetics.

For Mahāyāna the ideal of compassion was illustrated by the Buddha himself, who combined both the self-denial which led to enlightenment, and the life of service which followed. Instead of proceeding to Nirvāna, he spent forty years in compassion to mankind, and indeed has continued that activity ever since. In addition there are countless Bodhisattvas who are full of care and service for mankind. The twenty-fourth chapter of the Lotus Sūtra, which sings the praise and grace of Avalokiteśvara, is chanted daily by all schools, including Zen. Other Bodhisattvas are added, and other Buddhas, so that local deities or idealized personifications are easily included. Such are Amitābha or Amida in his Western Paradise, and Kwanyin or Kwannon, the Chinese and Japanese versions of Avalokiteśvara.

There are popular litanies which express the power and presence of these gracious beings, like that of the Chinese Hui-yen in his 'Song of the White Lotus of the Pure Land in the West'.

> There Amitābha stands in shining dress
> Preparing for the endless festival.
> He draws each human soul up from the abyss
> And lifts them into his palace of peace . . .
> Where they shine in the garden of redeemed spirits.[15]

Such communion with a Buddha, or deity, joins up with the mystical theism of devotional Hinduism and that of the Semitic religions. Communion takes the place of the identification of Brahman-ātman in monism, or the integration and isolation of Yoga or non-theistic Nirvāna.

Devotion to Buddhas and Bodhisattvas is characteristic of Pure Land schools of Mahāyāna Buddhism, though it affects all schools

[14] R. Gombrich, *Precept and Practice*, p. 322.
[15] Adapted from the translation by K. Reichelt in *Religion in Chinese Garment*, 1951, pp. 125 f.

to some extent, and it shows something of the potency of Buddhism as a fervent, all-embracing and communal religion. Even under the adversity of modern China the power of Buddhism to survive or revive should not be underestimated. It is not a mere ethic, but a religion which seeks mystical union.

Chapter 7

TAO AND SHINTO

CHINESE WAYS

Both China and Japan were profoundly influenced by Indian Buddhism and transformed it in their own ways. Yet they had their own mystical traditions which have persisted down the ages.

Whether Confucianism should be called religious has often been debated. Confucius himself was a kind of Chinese Socrates, intent on asking questions and teaching good behaviour. He did not found a religion, though he was soon regarded as the king of sages, the 'teacher of ten thousand generations', 'co-equal with heaven and earth', and in the early Christian period he was virtually deified. But Confucius himself would have been shocked by this adulation and not displeased at the reversion to his human status. Even under modern Communism the birthplace of Confucius has been redecorated at times, whilst at other times Confucian 'feudalism' has been reviled as contrary to the true doctrines of Chairman Mao, the 'never-dying Red Sun'.

Confucius, like Socrates, was religious in the broad sense of believing in a divine order that worked for good, in observing certain rituals, and in basing his ethical teaching on religious convictions. He spoke of Heaven (*t'ien*) in the sense of Nature or God and used common formulas which included the divine name. More profound, as with other Chinese thinkers, was his concern for the 'Way' (*Tao*), which is the principle by which things should be done or kingdoms ruled.

If it is the will of Heaven that the Way shall prevail, then the Way will prevail.

But if it is the will of Heaven that the Way should perish, then it must needs perish.[1]

The Way is the Way of Heaven, the ideal but natural order of the universe, and harmony and union with the Way brought harmony with all natural things. Confucius and his early followers were concerned with this world, and although he was attentive to ritual and respected the ancestors, he said, 'Until you know about the living, how are you to know about the dead?'[2] Yet he lived in an age of unrest and wars and clearly the Way of Man had gone astray from the Way of Heaven, so that he and his followers looked back to a golden age when men lived in virtue and harmony with Heaven and Earth.

The concept of the Way of Heaven was developed in the Doctrine of the Mean (*Chung Yung*), attributed to a grandson of Confucius. This taught a Mean or Middle Way, which emphasized good behaviour and the pervading power of Heaven and has been called 'religious and mystical'.[3] A great exponent of Confucianism, Mencius, was no more a religious founder than was Confucius, but it has been said that he is mystical in developing the doctrines of the Way of Heaven and righteousness. Mencius thought that human nature was essentially good, whereas Hsün Tzu thought it was evil, but both looked back to the original harmony of the Way of Man and the Way of Heaven. In so far as these Confucian beliefs were mystical they were naturalistic, or pantheistic at most, but clearer mystical ideas appear in the complex called Taoism.

Taoism has been called the real religion of China and, like the dragon whose tail can never be grasped, it is probable that Taoist ideas will survive the rationalism of modern times. The ethical and social concerns of Confucianism may be perpetuated in Communist or other social orders, and Maoism has been regarded as the modern

[1] *The Analects of Confucius*, tr. A. Waley, 1938, 14.38.
[2] Ibid., 11.11.
[3] W. T. Chan, *A Source Book in Chinese Philosophy*, 1963, pp. 95, 82.

state religion. But in personal experience Taoist and Buddhist teachings have long been effective.

Taoists have been called Quietists and condemned by critics as those who walk by themselves, think they are better than others, are of no real value, and would be better employed serving rulers or parents. Taoists would reply that the most useful practice was to cleanse oneself and so obtain truth and happiness, and above all power over self and the world. Many Chinese sought after that perfection which would come by stilling the appetites and emotions, and going back under the layers of toil and worry to the true self of 'man as he was meant to be'. Techniques were used like those of Indian Yoga, which consisted particularly in control of breath so that it became light and easy like that of a child or even that of a baby in the womb. Physical exercises were used, also as in Yoga, though some Taoists thought that these were too physical to be helpful for spiritual purposes.

Taoists sought to uncover the layers of consciousness so that they would arrive at pure consciousness, and see the inner truth of everything. This was regarded as the final truth and absolute bliss, and it gave power (*tê*) which enabled the quietist to dominate material things. In popular forms and legend Taoist practitioners, like wonder-working Yogis, sought to raise themselves from the ground, fly through the air, live on nothing, suspend breathing, indulge in wine or sexual powers, engage in magic and alchemy, and seek for the elixir of immortality and the islands of the blest.

Philosophical Taoism was more subtle and reserved. Early classics, the Tao Tê Ching and the Chuang Tzu, are not much concerned with immortality but rather with attaining peace and quiet. The truly wise man will discard conventional knowledge and banish normal human wisdom. Differently from the Confucians, the Taoists considered that established morality and wisdom prevented goodness rather than forming it.

> Banish wisdom, discard knowledge
> And the people will be benefited a hundredfold . . .
> Give them simplicity to look at,

the Uncarved Block to hold,
Give them selflessness and fewness of desires.[4]

The Taoist sought to return to the simplicity of the Uncarved
Block, the Great Concordance, the Great Way, the Mother of all
things, the original harmony of nature. He depended upon 'actionless
activity' (*wu wei*) and engaged in 'wordless teaching', and by giving
up he would gain power over all creatures. The aim was to cling to
quietness and push out into the Void, and none of the ten thousand
creatures would escape one's power. Goodness is like water which
does not scramble or seek the highest place, yet water overcomes
everything and benefits all creatures. The practice of Tao is to follow
the Way of Heaven, and a kingdom ruled by Tao would bring
contentment to everyone.

The Tao Tê Ching, the reputed work of Lao Tzu, teaches men to
'hold fast to the unity' which is the Tao that underlies and governs all
existence. In its basic and undivided unity all the contradictions and
distinctions of mortal life are resolved. All beings worship Tao and it
is called 'the mysterious power'. The sage renounces that he may
gain all, is bent so that he may become straight, is hollow that he may
become full.

> Those that have little, may get more,
> Those that have much, are but perplexed.
> Therefore the Sage
> Clasps the Primal Unity.[5]

Although the Tao Tê Ching sees the Tao as finally indescribable,
much of the book suggests that it can be known through mystical
intuition. Yet its teachings are not other-worldly, since the sage is
regarded as the ideal ruler.

But an interpretation of the Tao Tê Ching as a creed for hermits
who retire from public life seems to emerge from the second great
work of Taoism, attributed to Chuang Tzu, which in many stories of
sages and notables shows how they refused public office and

---

[4] A. Waley, *The Way and its Power*, 1934, p. 166.
[5] Tao Tê Ching, 22; *The Way and its Power*, p. 171.

preferred to retire to seclusion for self-cultivation. Chuang Tzu is almost indifferent to society and seeks not to reform but to rise above worldly troubles. He teaches individual freedom, not only from external restraints but also from the limitations of one's mind. He is a mystic in the sense that a man must live in the unity of the Tao, which is the absolute truth.

> You have a great tree and are worried about its uselessness. Why not plant it in the realm of Nothingness, in the expanse of Infinitude? Then you may sit by its side in actionless activity and lie under it in blissful Rest.[6]

Even the later Taoists probably never thought that all society would consist of ascetics, though they hoped for a return to an ideal state where there was peace and perfection. This would be under the guidance of wise men who governed without governing and encouraged goodness by discarding morality.

A basic Chinese concept is that of the two principles, Yin and Yang, feminine and masculine, darkness and light, which arose out of the undivided great Tao. These are comparable to Nature and Spirit in the Indian Sāmkhya system, and, as there, liberation comes through the isolation of the male Spirit from Nature, so in Taoism the return to the unity of Tao is through the male Yang. A famous Taoist text, *The Secret of the Golden Flower*, was expounded by the psychologist C. G. Jung to illustrate the process of integration.

> Our text gives us a metaphysical concept . . . which must be understood psychologically; it is the idea of the 'diamond body', the indestructible breath-body which develops in the Golden Flower.[7]

In the book itself the Golden Flower is Light and image, the true power of 'the transcendent Great One'. If the life-forces of the Yang are conserved, then man may reach to the stage of the Golden Flower which frees from the conflict of Yin and Yang, and he becomes once more part of Tao, the undivided Great One. This is a search for mystical unity, a monism or pantheism.

[6] Chuang Tzu, 1.
[7] *The Secret of the Golden Flower*, tr. R. Wilhelm and C. F. Baynes, 1931, p. 131.

TAO AND SHINTO

Taoist philosophers taught simplicity and tranquillity, which would lead to companionship with nature and unity with Tao. Popular movements, however, sought for the occult, in divination and magic, and the search for immortality. As the religion of the masses Taoism developed a great pantheon, with deities which represented historical and legendary persons as well as natural objects and forces. When Buddhism entered China, early in the Christian era, its priests and monks, temples and images, were imitated by Taoists. Secret societies were formed, which remained a feature of Taoism down to this century, when they are supposed to have been finally suppressed. Nowadays the outward forms of Taoist religion have disappeared, but the mystical attitudes of Taoism may remain under other guises.

Taoism has always been one of the sources of inspiration in art, and with its teaching of harmony with the Tao it is one of the great examples of nature mysticism. Chinese landscape painting, called 'mountain and water', and paintings of flowers and birds, reflect its viewpoints. Taoist writers put forward theories of painting to claim that it should not merely copy the outward forms of nature but embody its inner spirit, that spirit which unites man to nature in a mystical harmony which can still be felt in Chinese pictures. The naturalism and search for great powers led Taoists also into sexual adventures, which will be mentioned later.

All forms of nature could be glorified by Taoism; landscape painting came to be regarded not merely as a background for other subjects, but as itself expressing the harmony of Tao, and it became the crowning art of China.

Having embraced Tao the sage responds harmoniously to things. Having purified his mind, the worthy man enjoys forms. Landscapes exist in material substance and soar into the realm of the spirit. . . . Mountains and rivers in their form pay homage to Tao, and the man of humanity delights in them.[8]

---

[8] Tsung Ping, edn 1922, in W. T. de Bary, *Sources of Chinese Tradition*, 1960, p. 292.

MYSTICISM IN THE WORLD'S RELIGIONS

TAOIST–BUDDHIST SYNTHESIS

From its entry into China, about the first century A.D., Buddhism became closely associated with Taoism, and with Confucianism these came to be called 'three ways' rather than competing churches or 'isms'. There was occasional persecution of the foreign religion but over the centuries Buddhism became naturalized and assumed Chinese and Japanese dress. Buddhist religious themes mingled with Taoist naturalism in art, and Buddhist religious schools adapted themselves to Chinese expressions.

Devotion to Amitābha Buddha in his Pure Land in the West was very popular and provided a religion of personal adoration of supernatural beings. A deliberate synthesis was taught by the T'ient'ai (Heavenly Terrace) school, often called the Lotus since it used the Lotus Sūtra (but gave it a distinctively Chinese interpretation). Here Nirvāna is not extinction but the aim is to attain Buddhahood, and all beings will ultimately achieve that goal.

Nirvāna is not extinction, since all states are tranquil
and have no appearance.
When a son of Buddha has run his course
he becomes a Buddha in the next life . . .
There will be an infinite number of Buddhas
who will save all living beings . . .
and none will fail to become Buddha.[9]

Although generally known to the West as Zen, this school is a synthesis of Taoist and Buddhist thought. The origins are in the Chinese word Ch'an, which is supposed to be derived from Sanskrit *dhyāna*, 'meditation', and there are legends of the supposed founder Bodhi-dharma. But basically Ch'an is Chinese, the meditation-school, which shares with all forms of Buddhism the practice of meditation but has its own distinctive character in attaching exclusive importance to meditation as the truth in action as well as the means to final truth. While it used scriptural texts, Ch'an relied on intuition as the way to enlightenment and teaching passed on from 'mind to mind', from teacher to pupil without argument or

[9] Hui-ssu, ibid., pp. 352 f.

formal statement. Ch'an taught that the Buddha-nature is in all beings, and this is the essence of the Buddha-mind, which is empty of all distinctiveness and character. It criticized those who made offerings to Buddhist images for the sake of rewards and merit, and any deliberate aim, even seeking Nirvāna or Buddhahood, would be self-defeating. 'If one seeks for Buddhahood, the Buddha will become a cause of transmigration.' Rather by absence of deliberative thought, letting the mind take its course, meditators could arrive at the Void, which has no specific character.

Like other schools, Ch'an attributed its beginnings to the Buddha himself, the Buddha's smile, whereby he passed the teaching on to his disciple by simply holding up a flower and smiling. Some Ch'an masters taught 'absence of thought' in order to 'see one's original nature', and others emphasized intuition rather than rational knowledge. By enigmatic words and gestures, and illogical questions and answers, intuition was thought to be developed. This was considered to give true wisdom in a kind of monistic mysticism of union with the Buddha-nature or the Void.

SHINTO

Shinto is the Chinese term, Shen-Tao, for the Japanese 'Way of the Gods', and it is the ancient Japanese religion which, like Chinese Taoism, became strongly influenced by Buddhism. The superior powers of ancient Shinto were very diverse: natural, ancestral, heroic, fertility, magical. But characteristic of them all is the conviction that the gods (kami) are related to men and actually born of the same parents. For example the Sun Goddess, Amaterasu O-mi-kami, is not only a deity of nature but the ancestress of the royal house, as other spirits are of other families. Thus it is said that the same divine blood flows through plants, animals, men and gods. The universe is not inanimate but instinct with life, in which man shares and which he reveres at especially sacred places.

Shinto temples and their grounds express the kinship of man with nature and have an atmosphere of peace and spiritual refreshment. The sacred precincts are entered through formal gateways (torii), streams are crossed by bridges, there may be holy springs and fountains, fences or walls are passed to an inner shrine, and finally the holy place itself is reached. Unlike Buddhist temples, which are often great stone structures, Shinto shrines are small and simple. Some of the most sacred, like the national shrine of Amaterasu at Isé, are like log-cabins, made of unpainted wood with roofs of bark or tiles, and though they are ancient foundations they need renovation regularly. Only priests enter such small shrines, while for the laity there are worship halls for rituals and music. In the home the 'god-shelf' (*kami-dana*) has rice, salt and water placed on it every day, with fruit and other food on special occasions, thus affirming the presence of the spirits in everyday life.

With the arrival of Buddhism in the sixth century A.D. much of Shinto became submerged or absorbed. In India and China Buddhism had transformed some of the native gods, but the process went further in Japan where many temples and sacred places were taken over and a Dual Shinto (Ryobu) emerged. Buddhist images were regarded as representations of gods and Buddhist materials were used in worship. Shinto and Buddhist influences combined in painting and literature, and were manifested especially in the Japanese tea ceremony. Zen priests introduced tea to Japan and not only the beverage but the pottery in which it was served came from China for a long time, so that commercial as well as artistic interests were involved. The simple tea hut, with its garden, suggested both the closeness of nature and the bliss of Nirvāna. One of the Zen masters wrote, 'Drink tea to improve health and prolong life,' and the Lotus Sūtra was quoted as saying that 'everything finite tells of infinity'.[10]

A Shinto revival, from the eighteenth century, sought to separate it from Buddhism as the national religion. The absence of traditional scriptures, such as the Buddhists possessed, was felt keenly, new collections were encouraged and Shinto enthusiasts praised. the virtues of the national faith. The universality of the Sun Goddess was emphasized, but also her special favour for Japan.

The True Way is one and the same, in every country and throughout heaven and earth. This Way, however, has been correctly transmitted only in our Imperial Land. . . . One must

[10] R. Tsunoda, ed., *Sources of Japanese Tradition*, 1958, p. 263.

understand, first of all, the universal principle of the world. The principle is that Heaven and Earth, all the gods and all phenomena were brought into existence by the creative spirits.[11]

On the one hand Shinto was associated ever more closely with imperial activities, and on the other hand local shrines were developed. In every community there were shrines for the ancestors, and in many beauty spots and quiet places groves of trees and open land served both for quiet and for communal gatherings on special occasions. Many Shinto shrines to this day are small and placed in busy spots, but others are situated amid spacious surroundings which are conducive to calm and meditation. Popular worship turns to the gods as personal helpers, or to the Buddhas with the same purpose, while others seek a quieter mode of communion with the divine.

Many new religious movements have developed in Japan in modern times and from the nineteenth century a distinction was made between Shrine Shinto and Sect Shinto. These new religions have millions of followers and are of diverse origins. Some have centred on mountain pilgrimages, where trained leaders conduct groups of climbers and direct ecstatic experiences that come to them on the way or at attainment of the peaks of Mount Fuji or other heights. The Order of the Conic Peak is noted for the piety and asceticism of its members. Others engage in practices of divination, faith-healing and walking over burning charcoal in harmless peace.

More numerous are the Shinto sects which are organized like churches, with a charismatic founder and a strong communal organization involving a good deal of voluntary work for the society. The communal element appears further in the encouragement to lay participation in worship and the ecstatic behaviour which may be produced in it. Such movements often stress devotion in worship of the deity and calm which extends over all social and daily life.

The most popular of these new religions, the Tenri-kyō, has a 'mystical dance' at the centre of its ceremonies, which has been described by an onlooker.

[11] Motoori Norinaga Zenshu, 6.3; quoted in *Sources of Japanese Tradition*, pp. 520 f.

Here you notice no Oriental passivity or mental inertness, here no quietism nor inactivity, no calmful longing for yonder shore, no peaceful waiting for the light of *Amidabutsu*, no shaking off the human delusions and entering the path which will lead away from these restless, tossing waves of the ocean of life, to the rest of Nirvāna. . . . Here, in Tenrikyō's prayer, we do not move in a fleeting existence—on the contrary, one feels impulsive dynamics, energy, extreme zeal, effervescence, tenacity, unwavering determination with stream-lined movements.

After describing the movements of kimonos and fans, the positions of arms and fingers, the loud music and the sacred words, the writer continues:

All these things work together to create that indefinable mystical something which expresses itself on the faces of the Tenrikyō faithful when they speak about their religion or when they quote parts of this dancing psalm in ordinary conversation.[12]

[12] H. van Straelen, *The Religion of Divine Wisdom*, 1954, pp. 119 f.

Chapter 8

ASIAN AND AFRICAN ECSTATICS

SHAMANS

> It is difficult to find a religion which has not, at some stage in its
> history, inspired in the breasts of at least certain of its followers
> those transports of mystical exaltation in which man's whole being
> seems to fuse in a glorious communion with the divinity:[1]

So writes an eminent social anthropologist and he proceeds to
discuss many different religions, but especially those of illiterate
peoples and the Shamanism of Asia.

The word Shaman is perhaps derived from the Indian *samana* or
śramana, for a monk or ascetic. The Shaman of primitive peoples in
Asia has been described as primarily a Psychopomp, a leader of
souls, who is a master of experiences of ecstasy which are held to be
supreme expressions of religion. He may also be a priest, a poet, a
magician or a medicine-man, but the Shaman's chief concern is to
master traditional techniques by which he enters a state of ecstasy.
In such a trance he may be thought to fly through the air, or walk
unharmed through fire, and his soul is held to leave the body and rise
to the sky or descend to the underworld.

Throughout Asia, as well as in other continents, there are experts
in mystical trance, but there are also many more normal people who
experience calmer forms of communion with the divine. It has been
seen that the great historical and scriptural religions of India and the
Far East have some monistic philosophies which teach absorption

[1] I. M. Lewis, *Ecstatic Religion*, 1971, p. 18.

77

into the All, and on the other hand many popular cults of loving devotion to personal supernatural beings. There are also innumerable people who follow non-literary religious traditions, in India itself as well as other parts of central Asia and Siberia. Yet there are other elements of religion beside the Shamanic ecstasies, and not all ecstatics are Shamans since the latter are trained and expert rather than simply spontaneous. Shamanic experiences cover a wide range of activity and some of these are not strictly mystical, but when Shamans claim to be in communion with supernatural powers there is a clear link with mystics elsewhere. Siberian practices have been described in which the Shaman claims to ascend through heaven after heaven, to converse with the Supreme Creator, and receive secrets from him which may be communicated to others.[2]

Shamanism, like mysticism, has had confused interpretations because it has often been applied indiscriminately to practices of various kinds in many parts of the world, and Shamans have been identified with any sort of medicine-man or magician. Here we are only concerned to note that Shamans, and others, have some experiences which may be properly called mystical. The relationship of visions and raptures of other kinds to mysticism in general will be discussed later. Shamanic experiences may be the self-exaltation and impersonal identification of forms of monism, or they may be more theistic and imply communion with personal deities.

Shamanism has been described extensively in a standard work of that name by Mircea Eliade, in which he roams over Asia, Oceania, Australia and America, and those who are interested in such techniques among Altaians, Arunta, Andamanese, Apaches and others are referred to this and similar works. But Eliade says that he has omitted Africa, as that 'would lead us too far', and so more attention may be given to it here.[3]

AFRICAN MEDIUMS

African religion has long been ignored or misunderstood, and until recently many books on comparative religion had few or no

[2] M. Eliade, *Shamanism*. E. T. 1964, pp. 193 f.
[3] Ibid., p. 374n.

references to this continent, which still has probably over fifty million people who follow ancient African religions, as well as millions of others who are only partly Muslim or Christian. Yet attention has been given to the much smaller numbers who follow illiterate Asian, Australian or American religions.

To speak of mysticism in African tribal religions might seem absurd, though not to I. M. Lewis who considers 'the seizure of man by divinity' as the most profound of all religious experiences and one which is universal. Ecstasy and possession, if not Shamanistic flight, can be widely documented from Africa and in particular among those who receive training for such experiences.

Public manifestations of what may be called mysticism in Africa are found among those men and women who are thought, and think themselves, to be possessed by divine or ancestral spirits. There may be more normal and quiet forms of mysticism too, but most investigators have neglected the individual and inward side of religion and have concentrated upon outward display. Important studies of possession have been made, especially in West Africa, and in Dahomey and Togo the companies of ecstatic mediums are still well organized, though there has been decline elsewhere under modern pressures. The spirit in question is believed to be in such close communion with a man or woman that the person is possessed and becomes the servant or property of the divinity. In Dahomey it is said that the god 'enters the head' or 'mounts the head' of his servant. Indeed the union is so close that the person is called the 'wife of the god' (*vodun-si*), and he, or generally she, undergoes a course of training which aims at binding spirit and human being together in a sacred marriage.

In Nigeria, where organization of such people is less developed nowadays, the medium is also regarded as 'wife of god' (*iyawo-orisha*). Earlier writers who had heard of such god-wives thought that this involved a sexual connection and imagined heathen orgies. But the imagery of marriage is used here, as in other religions, to indicate the union of human and divine in terms of the closest human bond. The wife of the god receives messages from him and represents him publicly as his intermediary. The wife is passive in the state of trance, when it is held that the god speaks or performs dramatic actions, and at other times the god-wife has no special authority of her own.

Possession by the divinity often occurs spontaneously at first, probably at a public dance when others are possessed, though also in solitude, perhaps at home or in the forest when the subject shows a tendency to dissociation. The first possession may not last long but it may come more easily by repetition, or if it does not recur the person may return to normal life. Elsewhere I have described the training of mediums in communal 'god-houses'.[4] When a person is possessed he, or she, often falls to the ground as if dead. The body is carried away by attendants at the dance to the 'god-house' and there is brought back to life and trained for a new personality and new existence. This is a 'rite of passage' from an old life into a new, a rebirth into a divine communion, and a resurrection which takes place in the god-house but is publicly revealed only at the conclusion of a lengthy training. During this formation the devotee learns texts and songs belonging to the god, practises ecstatic possession under the guidance of an elder, and often learns a new language, which is the traditional tongue of the cult. The novice is frequently bathed with water and preparations of leaves to convey purity and power, and strengthen connection with the divinity. Finally the god-wife receives a new name, and is marked with tattoos on face, neck and shoulders, in traditional patterns of the god. The hair is often cut in characteristic ways, and necklaces and other ornaments and clothing indicate to the outside world to which god the medium belongs.

When the trained god-wives are eventually shown to the public there are great celebrations. Emerging from the god-houses, old and new devotees dance and sing before the crowds. Colourful costumes, and dramatic but controlled actions, indicate that union with the gods is complete. Some of the mediums remain attached to the temples, but others return to their homes and resume normal life. Either may be called upon by priests to go into trance states when consultations of the gods are required. There are regular and annual occasions, and other times of retreat, when the devotees return to the god-house for renewed activity and communion with the deity.

[4] Geoffrey Parrinder, *West African Religion*, 2nd edn, 1961, pp. 86 f.

Some of the regular possessions have been well described in Ghana, among the Gã and Ashanti. These trance states last two or three hours and are preceded by passive or dull states in the mediums. When drums begin beating the medium may shake or jump, and then call out, sing or prophesy in another language or unintelligible words. Mediums in states of possession often perform actions that would be difficult for them normally, such as running at great speed, whirling round like dervishes, or tearing off their clothes, though they are never completely naked. Often, however, possession takes quieter forms, with gentle shaking or dancing. The medium's face may have a mask-like impassivity, with the eyes staring fixedly or rolling about. The trance usually ends suddenly, with the medium falling to the ground, or throwing herself against a wall or into the arms of an assistant. She returns to her senses as though waking from deep sleep and may show surprise at her condition, but often she is tired and falls into real sleep.[5]

These ecstatics are often called 'mediums' and this is what they are, as intermediaries between men and gods and vehicles of divine beings which 'mount' or possess them. There is a similarity to the spiritualistic mediums of other lands who claim to be possessed by spirits of the dead, but these African mediums are thought to be possessed by other spirits, often tribal gods.

The trance states and abnormal behaviour of mediums have sometimes been compared with those of madmen, and this has suggested that they are hysterical or diseased. But the abnormality has its purposes. At the beginning of training the novice may seem to have lost his senses or be wandering in a vacant state, but this provides a receptivity, different from normal life with its controls, in which he can be taught the power and requirements of the god. Another authority, Pierre Verger, insists that the training seeks to create 'a mystical and unconscious dissociation (*dédoublement*) during which he will assume the traditional behaviour of the god'.[6] The primary experience is mystical and the messages from the god are not the cause but the product of possession. Similarly, the

[5] M. J. Field, *Religion and Medicine of the Gã People*, 1937; *Search for Security*, 1960, pp. 56 f.
[6] Pierre Verger, *Notes sur le Culte des Orisa et Vodun*, 1957, p. 71.

initiation of the medium does not aim mainly at revealing esoteric secrets but at creating a new personality in harmony with the divine.

Whether these mediums are hysterical, abnormal and therefore unreliable, has been debated. One writer urged doctors trained in the Western traditions of medicine to take more interest in religious studies. His own estimate was that ecstatic trances 'enter into the category of delirious interpretations, that is to say, statements which come from a real sensation, from a clear fact, of which only the conclusions are illogical or paranormal'. He held that 'these psychical troubles, whether provoked or not, are temporary', but he calls them both 'quasi-morbid states' and 'holy states'.[7]

But are they 'psychical troubles'? Margaret Field, who after her first anthropological field work trained in psychiatric medicine, came to different conclusions and provided far more details. She pointed out that cases of 'hysterical dissociation' which have been studied in Europe and America have been those of badly adjusted or really ill patients, and the interpretation often given to their hysteria was the wish to escape from heavy responsibility or difficult situations by taking refuge in a world of fantasy. But African mediums do not seek to escape from the world, and African religion, like Semitic, is strongly world-affirming. The medium goes into trance in order to participate in the nature and wisdom of the divinity, to bring its message to clients, and to help other people as well as herself.

Too much attention should not be given to the apparently abnormal behaviour of the ecstatic, which is not necessarily unusual in the context of the particular culture. Cries of ecstasy or joy, words in another or unknown language, symbolical actions and wild dances, are all expected signs of divine possession. Psychologists may interpret the messages of mediums or shamans as coming from the unconscious mind, but that is their point of view. From a theologian's standpoint this does not decide the authenticity of the revelation, or the honesty or normality of the medium. One may study the social, psychological and cultural aspects of an experience, but that does not give the clue to the experience itself as it appears to the recipient. The anthropologist I. M. Lewis is much more careful, and scientific:

[7] P. Maupoil, *La Géomancie à l'ancienne Côte des Esclaves*, 1943, pp. 60 f.

I certainly do not presume to contest the validity of their beliefs, or to imply, as some anthropologists do, that such beliefs are so patently absurd that those who hold them do not 'really' believe in them. My objective is not to explain away religion. On the contrary, my purpose is simply to try to isolate the particular social and other conditions which encourage the development of an ecstatic emphasis in religion.[8]

The normality and the social acceptability of the mediums need emphasis, since some critics might consider African religion to be largely the expression of a diseased mentality. Careful observers agree that the state of trance is temporary, that the trained mediums enter into it at will, that during this state the messages they give to their clients are helpful, and that the possession is for them the climax of union with the deity. The same would be said, of course, of ecstatics in other religions, such as Dervishes or Pentecostalists. African mediums not only seek to enjoy possession by spirits, they also try to help the clients who come for consultation in the crises of life. The bizarre actions and words are not unexpected by those who consult mediums, since the spirit world is considered to display superhuman powers.

Studies of possession have also been made among descendants of Africans in the Americas. The anthropologist M. J. Herskovits said that it was 'accepted as a perfectly normal experience by many people', which the religious atmosphere encouraged throughout life. 'From childhood the person had been taught that he could or was likely to receive one of the divinities, and that the gods are called up by means of drum beats and regular songs'; these produced a receptive mind and therefore 'the response is not delayed and possession takes place'.[9] Another anthropologist, R. Bastide, writes in similar tone: 'The mystical crisis is not produced by chance, and it does not create its own ritual as happens with diseased people; it is part of a cultural environment.' After careful examination he concludes that 'trance is a phenomenon of pressure by society and not a nervous phenomenon'. Because it is expected as the channel of

[8] I. M. Lewis, *Ecstatic Religion*, p. 28.

[9] M. J. Herskovits, *Pesquisas Ethnologicas na Bahia*, 1941, quoted in P. Verger, *Notes sur le Culte des Orisa et Vodun*, pp. 75 f.

spiritual power, 'a mystical manifestation which begins at a given moment . . . can only be explained by the preliminary effect of society on the mystic'.[10]

In another work Bastide gave other explanations of the mysticism of African and American negro mediums, insisting on their normality and social functions. He distinguished the possessing powers of the mediums, their controls, as either ancestors or natural forces and concluded that this gave them a mystical participation with spirits of earth, water, fire, minerals and the like. This, thought Bastide, produced an immanental mysticism, of the earth, but it was different from Christian mysticism, which is of the heavens and ascensional. There seems to be no African mysticism of God because although a Supreme Being is widely believed in, he is thought to be far away and he has no general worship or places dedicated to him.[11] Therefore the possessing powers are theoretically subordinate to the Supreme Being, though they may be High Gods in their own right. Moreover, these are personal spirits, which manifest their own characteristics in their mediums. Not all belong to the earth, some of the most popular are storm and celestial spirits, and most of them have not only supernatural but transcendental personalities ascribed to them. If polytheism is a form of theism, these mediums are theistic rather than monistic mystics.

The African mediums, it has been stressed, are not isolated or abnormal individuals, but they must be understood in their cultural environment. The spirits which are believed to possess them are those worshipped by communities, sometimes in particular localities, sometimes over wide areas with many temples. Something of the experience of the medium may be felt by more ordinary people, since dreams, visions and supernatural experiences are taken for granted and are not the exclusive possession of a restricted class. The states of ecstasy which Marghanita Laski found to be common among her friends are common currency in Africa as in many other lands.

Unhappily studies of African religion are seriously hampered by

[10] R. Bastide, *Imagens do Nordeste Mistico*, 1945, in Verger, loc. cit; and R. Bastide, *African Civilisations in the New World*. E. T. 1971, p. 101.

[11] R. Bastide in *Réincarnation et Vie Mystique en Afrique Noire*, ed. D. Zahan, 1965, p. 140.

lack of documents. Since there was no writing, there are no historical scriptures to express the faith from the inside, and virtually all our knowledge comes from outside observers. These are mostly foreign to the country, and those educated Africans who have begun increasingly to study the religion of their forefathers are conditioned by their education to a largely Western approach, and many of them are Christian ministers. The situation is even more serious in the field of ordinary religious experience and expression. There are virtually no spiritual autobiographies compiled from the inside, to reveal the feelings and aspirations of the common man. Some modern novels, such as those of Amos Tutuola, are attractive because of the worlds of dream and fantasy which they reveal, and they are based on popular ideas, but they are fiction rather than religious narrative.

It is unlikely that accounts of the religious experience of ordinary people in traditional Africa will be obtained from the inside at this late date, but in many ways the Independent churches continue the religion of the past. These are formally Christian bodies, separated from the mission churches, generally orthodox in doctrine but traditionally African in many customs. The very popular organizations of African Christian 'Mothers', Manyanos, have been well described in their religious services.

> The air is heavily charged with emotion. Women stand up and speak out their troubles, sometimes wailing or screaming, sometimes in frenzied whisperings. Their bodies tremble. Their eyes are tightly closed or fixed heavenwards. Talk is of miracles, of the sick and the dead . . . until one will start shaking violently in preparation for the moment when 'she is taken by the Spirit' and begins to speak. The other women listen intently, in close participation, and while the speaker slowly works herself up to a high pitch of emotion, the feelings of the listeners find in her a channel through which they pour themselves out, and by so doing generate again renewed tension in the individual who acts as a focus of, and outlet for, the collective mood.[12]

More westernized critics tell the women that the spirit which speaks through them is not the Holy Spirit but a demon, but 'they do

[12] M. Brandel-Syrier, *Black Woman in Search of God*, 1962, pp. 34 f.

not believe it' and laugh heartily. There are leaders of these churches, often called prophets and prophetesses, or apostles and bishops, but the possessions to which some of them are subject can be experienced by many others who have no formal rank in the organization. If it is a mystical experience it seems to spread through the whole community.

Some African writers have criticized the Independent churches, not for mysticism but, surprisingly, for their concentration upon the material needs of their followers. 'The "spiritual churches", highly sensitive to the most pressing needs of their people, tend to be restricted in their entire purview by these very needs.'[13] The special rites, ecstatic dances and possessions are considered to have overriding material aims. There is undoubted faith, but it is said to be subordinate to works. At least this religion is not world-denying but, in the general African tradition, world-affirming in its mystical possession.

On the other hand, the Independents criticize the mission or historical churches as themselves so materialistic that they have 'quenched the Spirit'. The missions have turned a great deal of energy to organization, education and social activities, and they are attacked for thinking about influence and position rather than the experience of the Spirit. If it is true that spiritual experience is more fundamental to religion than belief or ritual, then the Independents put the emphasis in the right place. Both in being 'taken by the Spirit' and in general experience there are expressions of the mystical life.

[13] C. G. Baëta, *Prophetism in Ghana*, 1962, p. 146.

PART III

Mystical Theism

Chapter 9

INDIAN MONOTHEISM

MONIST AND THEIST

In Indian and other philosophies monistic self-identification has flourished but there have constantly appeared contrary tendencies of personal relationships with spirits or deities. This has been the rule on the popular level, for philosophical abstractions have been felt inadequate for religions that had to face the struggles of everyday life. Even the ethics and negations of Buddhism were enriched with positive religious devotions. It seems to have been as Oliver Edwards told Dr Johnson, 'I have tried too in my time to be a philosopher; but, I don't know how, cheerfulness was always breaking in.'

It was not merely a vulgar crowd that needed a personal God, or crude Western religions that made God in their own image. Some of the most refined Asian scriptures, in India and beyond, came to proclaim a God of grace, with whom men sought communion but not identity. Such doctrines appear both in popular scriptures and in philosophical expositions. For if there is identity of the one with the all, in the sense that not only individuality but any distinction is an illusion, then the soul is God and God is the soul. Personality is annihilated or realizes that existence is only the universal existence. The world itself is probably also unreal, absolutely non-existent, since there is only one true unmanifested being. Good and evil disappear, since all is one. And if everything is the same this means tautology, whatever is exists, or non-exists, and nothing more can be said. This would be the death of discussion, and even more of religion.

The theist does not, or need not, condemn monism so much as find it unsatisfactory for himself and the facts of life. It seems not only to devalue the world and human dignity, but even more to devalue God. And, to him, it devalues mystical experience, which for a theist is a personal communion. It originates in an act of grace which is not simply a divine response but a primary action initiated by God. To say that a theistic mystical experience is the same as a monistic one would seem to him a misinterpretation of what each mystic claims to have experienced. The theist need not deny the validity of the monistic experience, but he might suggest that it has been incorrectly ascribed to the monist himself, whereas on his own theology all true religious experience comes from God. As the Bhagavad Gītā puts it:

> To this or that form devotees
> present their worship, having faith,
> yet I myself will allocate
> to everyone unswerving faith. (7.21)

It is appropriate to turn to Indian monotheism, since Indian monism and comparable theories have been considered. Moreover, it used to be customary to separate religions as Eastern and Western, or Indian and Semitic, and further distinguish them as Wisdom and Prophetic, or Mystical and Theistic. But India has had its own powerful forms of monotheism, and its solutions of the problems of diversity in the divine being are as striking as those of Hebrew and kindred faiths.

WORLD-AFFIRMATION AND MĀYĀ

Mysticism has been criticized as other-worldly, the mystic reducing himself to inactivity. Such attacks have been made especially against Indian mysticism, whose apparent world-denial has been thought to come both from a monistic philosophy and from a popular religion which seeks union with divine beings beyond this world. Christianity, on the contrary, at least in non-mystical forms, is supposed to be this-worldly, a form of socialism if not an ally of scientific materialism. Therefore some writers have considered that mysticism is unnatural within a Christian context, though even more so in Judaism and Islam.

The famous sociologist Max Weber maintained that the failure of India to win the race for modernization was due to its irrational and ecstatic religion, which could not accept the rationalization of life and the benefits of 'the spirit of capitalism'. Weber, who was one of those who have written about India without ever visiting it, held that because of its mysticism India was 'unable to take over the economic and technically finished form as an artifact, as occurred in Japan'.[1] Yet this opinion did not take into account the apparent other-worldliness of Japanese Buddhism, the nature-mysticism of Shinto, and the modern salvation-sects, which have not hindered Japan from taking a prominent part in the world-affirmations of capitalism.

It is astonishing that those who blame an ethereal philosophy or an ecstatic religion for modern economic difficulties, which have quite other causes, should not consider the achievements of the past which developed under similar religious influences. Only total ignorance of the great civilizations that have flourished in India, the exuberance of architecture and sculpture, painting and poetry, music and dance, the enjoyment of life and love, that appear again and again over the centuries—only such ignorance, or wilful blindness, could explain the refusal to face the facts of Indian religion and its relation to the lively material cultures.

Other students of Indian religion have felt that the closer their acquaintance with documents and practices has become, the more doubts have grown whether India has been dominated by the idea of world-negation. Such negation has been one element, notably among forest ascetics, but how influential has it been in important philosophies and in general religion? At least it seems that affirmation of the world and life has been powerful, parallel to the world-denial of hermits, from the early stages of Indian thought. Indeed the co-existence and subtle inter-weavings of negation and affirmation are among the special characteristics of Indian philosophy and religion.

It is unfortunate that Western interpreters have given the impression that Indian classics teach *māyā*, in the sense of the illusoriness of the world. The *Concise Oxford Dictionary* bluntly

[1] M. Weber, *The Religion of India*. E.T., 1958, p. 325.

defines 'māyā' as 'illusion', and the complete dictionary traces its appearance in English to Colebrook's dictum in 1827 of 'the notion that the versatile world is an illusion'. Yet even for monistic philosophers *māyā* is only an illusion from the viewpoint of the absolute Reality, while in the empirical world it is real.

Māyā occurs many times in the Rig Veda for extraordinary or supernatural powers (related to English 'measure'), and by extension it can be used of artifices, deceits and magic. But it is rare in the philosophical Upanishads. We read of 'Indra by his magic powers going about in many forms', while one of the only verses that could be interpreted in an illusory sense reads 'Nature is *māyā*', or '*Māyā* is material nature', and the wielder or possessor of *māyā* is 'the mighty Lord'.[2]

This is the identification of the Nature (*Prakriti*) of Sāmkhya teaching with *māyā* as divine power, and so both *māyā* and Nature are terms for the material world. There is no suggestion here that the world is illusory, though some commentators have thought so, and the important fact that this verse occurs in the most theistic of the classical Upanishads shows that *māyā* must be subject to God. The Upanishads in general are concerned with the reality within all things and do not suggest the illusory character of the world.

A similar usage of *māyā* is in the Bhagavad Gītā and this is especially significant in the interpretation of key passages, such as those which indicate the coming of the divine Avatar. So it is declared that 'by my own power (or creative energy, *ātma-māyayā*) I come to be in time'. This event is clearly considered to happen by divine decision and might and it is by no means an illusion, though some English translators have thoroughly weakened the sense by rendering it as 'illusion'.[3]

---

[2] Brihad-āranyaka Upanishad, 2.5.19. Śvetāśvatara Upanishad, 4.10. R. Reyna, in *The Concept of Māyā*, 1962, p. 7, interprets this verse as 'cosmic illusion', but a more careful exposition is made by P. D. Devanandan, *The Concept of Māyā*, 1950, pp. 57 f.

[3] Bhagavad Gītā, 4.6. Some translators render this 'magic' or 'illusion', and even W. D. P. Hill's translation (1928) gives 'my delusive power'. F. Edgerton (1944) renders *māyā* here as 'mysterious power' but on 7.14 he gives 'trick-of-illusion', perhaps following Rāmānuja who gave 'tricky arguments'.

INDIAN MONOTHEISM

Further in the Gītā we read that 'all this is my divine *māyā*', but those who trust in God alone shall 'pass beyond this *māyā*'.[4] It seems here to be following the Śvetāśvatara Upanishad and identifying *māyā* with 'material Nature'. The Gītā regards Nature as real, the product of divine creative power. Yet it is hard to transcend because the constituent qualities of Nature blind men to ultimate reality and they cling to a lower state, if they do not trust in God. Hence Nature (or *māyā*) is 'demonic' if it blinds men to God, but it is 'divine' if it is understood to be dependent upon God and the very manner of his worldly action.

The Bhagavad Gītā is the classic defender of moral activity in the world, yet it is also a mystical treatise. It states categorically that perfection does not come by simply renouncing actions, and that nobody is able to live on earth without engaging in some activity, for the very constituent qualities of Nature force him to it. The Gītā is bitingly critical of those ascetics who renounce worldly activities but still meditate on sensual things, and it declares that it is the duty of every man to do his own proper work. This human activity is further justified in a remarkable picture of the divine actions. God does not have to act in order to gain anything, as if he were lacking it, and he is not forced to act by the entail of *karma* (4.22). But God is always at work sustaining the world, which would perish without his maintenance. Hence man must act, following the divine example and the model of great men of old, and he must work for the benefit of the world. Such teaching continues throughout the Gītā.

Criticism of the Gītā has come from a surprising quarter in an assertion that the murderer Charles Manson believed that mystical realization of the Absolute dispensed him from the obligations of morality, and that the famous Gītā verse 'He kills not, is not killed' (2.19) is a dangerous doctrine if mystical experience means the achievement of a timeless moment in which all action is seen to be ultimately illusory.[5] It must be admitted that even some modern commentators suggest a cold asceticism, and an illustrated commentary quotes an earlier verse 'The wise lament neither for the living nor the dead' (2.11), and gives a picture of a yogi marching rapt

[4] Gītā, 7.14.
[5] R. C. Zaehner, *Our Savage God*, 1974, pp. 89 etc.

and uncaring past the poor, crippled and dying.[6] But both these verses need to be taken in context, which is the assertion of the immortality and indestructibility of the soul.

It must suffice here to repeat that the Gītā affirms the reality of the world, under God, that it teaches the importance of action in the world, and also that union with God is the height of its mysticism. Not only does the devotee 'see God in everything and everything in God', but finally he comes to know who God is, in very truth, enters into him immediately, and, performing all actions by the divine grace, will finally reach the eternal and changeless state.

MONOTHEISTIC MYSTICISM IN THE GĪTĀ

The Bhagavad Gītā succeeded to the diverse teachings of the Upanishads, Sāmkhya-Yoga and Buddhism. It is an astonishing synthesis, weaving many strands together, yet with a dominant and fervent monotheism. At an early stage (2.61) the Gītā tells the man of action to abandon desires, to control his senses, and to be intent on the Lord. It proceeds to teach the Meditation-Yoga, directed to God, of which we have spoken.

Like a monist, the Gītā sees all things abiding in the Supreme Being, as the wind penetrates the universe. And yet the divine being is not held by other beings, and they are not really in him, for he is incomparably greater.

> Yet beings do not rest in me,
> behold my sovereign activity!
> Support of beings yet not in beings
> is my Self that causes things to be. (9.5)

In a long catalogue in chapter ten, Krishna is identified with the chief of all classes of beings. He is the soul in all beings, the sun among all lights, the Himalayas among all mountains, the ocean among all waters, and so on. He is even his hearer Arjuna, though the reverse is not stated and Arjuna is never identified with God. This is different from monistic teaching, and there is no 'Thou art That'.

The mystical knowledge of the devotee recognizes God in everything.

[6] A. C. Bhaktivedanta, *Bhagavad-Gītā As It Is*, 1972, plate 7.

> The man who sees me everywhere,
> discerning everything in me,
> I am not ever lost to him
> and he is never lost to me. (6.30)

But a further development comes with the transcendental and terrifying vision of chapter eleven, perhaps the most detailed vision of God in all religious literature. Here, in 'the splendour of a thousand suns', all the gods appear in the body of the Supreme Being, who is the primal God, the eternal Spirit, greater than Brahman itself. Arjuna is frightened at this vision, which fills the universe with fire and portends the dissolution of the ages. He confesses his negligence and sin at over-familiarity with the embodied deity and asks forgiveness. Here it is transcendence, rather than immanence, which leads to grace and love. At his disciple's fear Krishna bows down, takes back his old human form, and comforts his friend. Here love is emphasized, the love of man for God but also the love of God for man.

There can be no love in soul-isolation, and monistic identification precludes the subject-object relationship which love requires. But chapter twelve of the Gītā says that the way of love (*bhakti*) is the easiest and best of ways, and it is superior to the hard toil of those who seek the abstract Absolute.

> For hardly can the embodied soul
> attain the unmanifested goal. (12.5)

Bhakti, devotion and love, comes from a root which means to share or participate, and increasingly it means to participate with affection in something or someone. It is used of sexual love, never in the Gītā though in some later forms of the worship of Krishna. It is used first in the Gītā of human love for the Lord, and then of divine love for man. In this pure sense of religious love *bhakti* in the Gītā is comparable to *agapé* in the New Testament, though in later Krishna cults *bhakti* is often more akin to the Greek *eros*.[7]

In the Gītā man is exhorted to love God, before all sacrifices,

[7] R. C. Zaehner, *The Bhagavad-Gītā*, 1969, p. 181; M. Dhavamony, *Love of God according to Śaiva Siddhānta*, 1971, pp. 15 f.

austerities and scriptures. And, best of all, God loves man. In six successive verses at the end of chapter twelve, man is called dear to God and finally exceedingly dear.

In the final chapter of the Gītā a man who is freed from all desire and egotism is said to be fit for becoming Brahman, the goal of the monists. But the Gītā's theism cannot leave matters there. Having become Brahman, that is perfect, the fully integrated man goes on to attain supreme love of God and full union with him.

> By love he comes to recognize
> my greatness, who I really am
> and enters into me at once
> by knowing me as I really am. (18.55)

Such union is achieved by divine grace, which both gives strength for doing one's duty and provides freedom from attachment, and the attainment of an eternal and unchanging state of bliss with God. The combination of action and devotion is characteristic of the Gītā and at the end its highest message, the greatest mystery of all, is that man is 'greatly loved' (*ishto*) by God, who is the only refuge of the soul and communion with whom is the highest bliss.

> Go to him alone for refuge
> with all your being, by his grace
> you will attain the highest peace
> and his eternal resting place. (18.62)

The Gītā is both a mystical and a practical document of the highest order. It teaches union with God, but in the context of love to God and love from God, which implies some distinction of subject and object. Its God is fully and solely God, not an ordinary soul, and not a 'god of one's choice' or a temporary Lord to provide help on the road to isolation. The Gītā scorns formal ritual, repetition of texts, ascetic practices and giving alms to priests. It insists on proper action, doing one's duty in the world, first by working without hope of rewards, and then by acting intent on God and going to him alone. Krishna is God in the full sense of creator of the universe and its dissolver, above all gods and the neuter Brahman, yet manifested in the world from time to time in a human form. Communion with God in the closest sense, in him though not containing him, shows a theistic mysticism of unity without identity.

PHILOSOPHICAL EXPOSITION OF THE GĪTĀ

It has been seen (page 38) that Śankara gave a monistic interpretation to the Upanishads and the Gītā, and he is unsatisfactory when dealing with important theistic elements in the Gītā, the divine birth and the terrifying transfiguration. About the eleventh century A.D. the philosopher Rāmānuja came much closer to the spirit of the Gītā in his commentary on it and in other writings. Rāmānuja and his followers are particularly important, for not only were they and do they remain very influential, but they disprove a common notion that all Indian philosophy is thoroughly monistic, and that monism is necessarily the highest form of mysticism.

Rāmānuja set out deliberately to criticize and change the monistic doctrines of Śankara, which he saw to threaten true religion and worship. In its tendency to depreciate both grace and works, monism ran the dangers of quietism and immoralism. Many other Indian teachers and poets developed theistic mysticism, but Rāmānuja was especially important in providing philosophical theory and justification for the devotional movements of his day and later. Indeed in the history of religions this theistic reaction is most significant, for whereas Western theologians may turn to immanence in revulsion against extreme transcendentalism, Indian theism turned in the opposite direction against monism.

Rāmānuja, like most Indians, held that the soul is eternal, but he thought that it is of the same substance as God. Yet all souls are not one, for there are many individuals. Moreover, while these souls have a mystical union with God, they can be differentiated from him.

> The Supreme Spirit must be understood to be in a different category from all souls, whether bound or liberated. For 'it is he who has entered the three worlds and sustains them' [Gītā 15.17]. . . . He who is of imperishable nature, must be in a different category from both non-intelligent matter which is perishable, from the intelligent [soul] which is bound to conform to matter because it is bound up with it, and from the liberated

MYSTICISM IN THE WORLD'S RELIGIONS

[soul] which was formerly involved in it because such involvement in unconscious matter is natural to it.[8]

Adopting an ancient mythological description of the emergence of all beings from the body of Vishnu at the beginning of a world cycle, Rāmānuja, who often speaks of God as Vishnu rather than Brahman, holds that the eternal souls form part of the body of God. They come into bodies, not in an illusory manner as some thought, but by the real action of God working in the world. Then at the end of the world-cycle they are reabsorbed into the body of the deity.

Commenting on the verse of the Gītā which says that God dwells in the heart of all beings, Rāmānuja remarks that they form the divine body as he is their soul. As the soul of all beings God is their beginning, middle and end, the cause of the origin of beings, of their continued existence and of their passing away from the world.

Armed with a doctrine called 'qualified non-dualism' (*viśisht-ādvaita*) or 'difference-non-difference' (*bhed-ābheda*), personal mystical theism emerged, because, like the Gītā, Rāmānuja concentrated upon the God of love. A man who has great love for God cannot continue to exist without him. For God is 'an ocean of boundless compassion, moral excellence, tenderness, generosity, and sovereignty, the refuge of the whole world without distinction of persons'. Through the divine love man becomes aware that God alone is the true goal of all his striving, and so love is the key to the relationships of man and God.

But Rāmānuja goes even farther than the Gītā. Not only does man need God, and God love man, but man is necessary to God, as his body. He is needed by God for loving communion.

> Just as my devotee who approaches me as his ultimate goal cannot maintain himself in existence without me, so too I cannot maintain myself without him. Thus he is my very soul. . . . Whoever loves me beyond measure, him will I love beyond measure in return. Unable to endure separation from him, I cause him to possess me.[9]

[8] Rāmānuja's Commentary on the Bhagavad Gītā, on verse 15.17; tr. R. C. Zaehner in *Hindu and Muslim Mysticism*, 1960, p. 194.

[9] Rāmānuja on Gītā, 7.18, and 18.65; from R. C. Zaehner, *Hindu and Muslim Mysticism*, p. 197.

DEVELOPING MYSTICAL THEISM

Mystical devotion to a personal God developed in many ways during the two thousand years since the composition of the Bhagavad Gītā. The mythology of Krishna was developed in other parts of the Mahābhārata, and in later works like the Harivamśa, 'the family of Hari' (Vishnu-Krishna). Some ten or more Avatars of Vishnu are detailed, with particular attention to Krishna, his miraculous though not virginal birth, childhood, youth, manhood and exploits, which are part of his divine 'play' (*līlā*). Interest centres on Krishna's life among the cowherds and adventures with the milkmaids (*gopīs*). He dances with them and each one thinks that he is dancing with her alone. This is a symbol of union with God wherein 'all acts of merit were effaced by rapture', and it became a favourite theme in later mystical works.[10]

Among the Purānas, 'ancient tales', the most popular is the Bhāgavata Purāna, of perhaps the ninth or tenth century, and known for its stories even more fondly than the intellectualist Bhagavad Gītā. The Bhāgavata Purāna has curiously monistic tendencies in its theory, though it does not appear to be connected with the schools of either Śankara or Rāmānuja. Yet it had a great influence on later theistic mystics who rejected monism, like Chaitanya. The Purāna lists twenty-two divine Avatars but gives most space to Krishna, who is the Lord himself, the Supreme Spirit. The divine sport takes place with the milkmaids of Brindāban and erotic symbolism is used. Krishna steals the clothes of the bathing girls and makes them appear naked before him, which is taken as the nakedness of the soul before God. He calls the young women to leave their husbands, as souls must leave all for God. He is their most 'beloved Lord' and they join him with eyes glowing with love.[11]

Not named in this Purāna but soon appearing in other works is one cowgirl, Rādhā, who becomes Krishna's paramour and came to be regarded as an Avatar of Lakshmī, consort of Vishnu. Many poets wrote of the loving relationships of Krishna and Rādhā as God and the soul in the closest union. There is love, absence, estrangement, a dark night of the soul in despair, and final rapturous

[10] See my *Avatar and Incarnation*, 1970, pp. 71 f.   [11] Ibid. pp. 74 f.

reunion. In the twelfth century Jayadeva, a Bengali poet, wrote in Sanskrit the Gīta Govinda, 'The Song of the Cowherd'. Here Rādhā sings of her love for Krishna and laments his fondness for other women, while Krishna fears that her love may be destroyed through his apparent inconstancy. He goes to her and pleads for a reconciliation and after appeals from others there is final reunion and union described in sensual words.

> Their love play grown great was very delightful, the love play where thrills were a hindrance to firm embraces,
> Where their helpless closing of eyes was a hindrance to longing looks at each other, and their secret talk to their drinking of each the other's nectar of lips, and where the skill of their love was hindered by boundless delight.[12]

Here *agapé* has become *eros* and mysticism is depicted in terms of sensual union, but the relationship of lover and beloved demands some distinction of subject and object. Theism, but hardly logical monism, is demanded by such love-mysticism.

Many poets took up this theme, and the love of Krishna and Rādhā has remained popular. Vidyāpati in the fifteenth century used many images to express the divine-human love.

> The moon and the night-lily
> Unite in love . . .
> I saw Krishna everywhere.[13]

Chandi Dās in the following century, a rebel poet-priest of Bengal, used similar terms.

> Who could ever wish me to leave my loving,
> I would rather eat poison than hear such words.
> I have explored his beauty and found no shores,
> But the god at last is standing by me.
> I will fulfil my dream and let the rest go.[14]

Such love poetry was particularly strong in Bengal, but in other

[12] Gīta Govinda XII, 1, tr. G. Keyt, 1947.
[13] *Love Songs of Vidyāpati*, tr. D. Bhattacharya, 1963, p. 79.
[14] *Love Songs of Chandidās*, tr. D. Bhattacharya, 1967, p. 102.

parts of India also mystical writers flourished, and a favourite was
Mīra Bāi, a princess of Rajputana in the west, who fled from home
after the death of her husband and became a *bhakta* devotee,
composing hymns in praise of Rādhā-Krishna and regarding herself
as the bride of Krishna. In the darkness of separation she sang:

> Mīra's heart is set on Hari.
> For lack of the vision of him my eyes are aching.
> Ah, my Lord, ever since thou hast been separated
> from me my heart has found no rest.[15]

In southern India there was a strong movement of devotion to
Vishnu under the form of Krishna, inspired by the poetry of twelve
devotees, Ālvārs, from the seventh to the tenth centuries, and these
helped in the revival of Hinduism among the Tamil people, a theistic
reaction against the currents of Buddhism and Jainism. Devotional
hymns in Tamil are sung both popularly and in temples, alongside
recitation of Vedic texts in Sanskrit.

The works of the Bengali poets were largely individual and
literary, and perhaps even more interested in erotic love than in
religious devotion. They did not found religious movements, but the
Ālvārs did and they are important communally as well as in
teaching. The Ālvār hymns do not mention Rādhā and are not erotic,
but they do make important identifications of the devotees with the
milkmaids, Gopīs, and others in the Krishna story. This provided a
direct participation of the devotee in the stories of the Lord and was
perhaps a new element in religious development. A favourite hymn,
by a poetess Āndāl, pictures her as one of the Gopīs rousing the
sleeping Krishna.

> We go to the jungle with the cows
> and eat there, as cowherds knowing nothing,
> yet this is our great gift that among us
> you were born—you who lack nothing.[16]

[15] Mīra-bāi, Bhajan, LIII, tr. Mrs Taylor and R. M. Nilkanth, in *Poems by Indian Women*, 1923.
[16] Adapted from J. S. M. Hooper, *Hymns of the Ālvārs*, 1929, p. 57.

Identification with figures from Krishna legends, which is not found in the Purānas, came to be important in an outstanding Bengali of the sixteenth century, Chaitanya. Although he lived long after the Ālvārs, it has been argued that they alone provided the communal religious inspiration which enabled the theory of divine-human union to be translated into practice.[17]

Chaitanya gave many emotional expressions to his religious devotion and mystical union by identification. In early life he fell into trances, which were first thought to be insanity but became accepted as absorption into the deity. By music, dancing and acting he expressed the love of Krishna and Rādhā. He often acted the part of Rādhā, dressed as a woman, experiencing her agony of separation from Krishna and the bliss of reunion.

Chaitanya attracted followers who joined in song-dances, *kīrtans*, and processions which enacted episodes from the Krishna-Rādhā story and called men to devotion. He visited the ruined Krishna centre at Brindāban and thanks to his inspiration it was rebuilt and remains to this day a great place of pilgrimage. Chaitanya himself came to be regarded as an Avatar of Krishna, and Rādhā and Krishna were claimed to be two and yet one, manifested in the body of Chaitanya. He taught love (*prema*) of a highly emotional kind, expressed in dance and song, crying and fainting, and he may have died by drowning in a fit of ecstasy in the sea near the temple of Krishna at Purī.[18]

The passionate love of God inspired by Chaitanya and others strengthened the devotional movements and has many followers to this day. About two million pilgrims go every year to Brindāban, the place of the love-play of Krishna and the milkmaids, and Mathurā his birthplace. A recent observer, a Roman Catholic priest who spent two years there joining in the processions, describes a scene.

They sang their bhajans, beating the time with drums and cymbals. The clear and loud voices of the little children and the harsher, deeper ones of the men, the strong voices of the village

[17] F. Hardy, 'Mādhavêndra Purī: A link between Bengal Vaishnavism and South Indian Bhakti', *Journal of the Royal Asiatic Society*, 1974, pp. 23 f.
[18] See my *Avatar and Incarnation*, pp. 82 f.

women and the reserved, soft voices of the genteel ladies—all of them sang the praises of Krishna and Radha and all of them went this way in search of greater love for him, perhaps even to behold him in reality.[19]

In the Western world we have become accustomed to the sight of yellow-robed young men and women singing and playing musical instruments, selling books and chanting 'Hare Krishna'. Since many of their converts seem to be young American men and women it is a significant indication of the appeal of theistic and emotional religion today, and a change from the more intellectualist and often agnostic attraction of philosophical Vedānta and Buddhism some years ago. The mystical, in the sense of union with a personal God, still has a great appeal in many countries.

RĀMA AND THE NAME

There were other developments of theism among the followers of Vishnu. In doctrine one school taught the 'cat-rule', complete surrender to God as the only way of receiving his grace, as a cat picks up kittens by its teeth without any effort on their part. But the 'monkey-rule' teaching said that salvation can only be obtained by some effort from the believer, as a young monkey clings to the body of its mother. These doctrinal divisions have been compared with Calvinism and Arminianism in Christianity.

Rāma was an incarnation, or God himself, just as important as Krishna or even more so to many believers. The worship of Rāma has been free from that eroticism that has marked so much of the later Krishna cult, but on the other hand there appear tendencies again to monism in more abstract contexts. Rāma may have been a historical king, and is regarded as such by his worshippers, being the deity incarnate. His story appears first in the Mahābhārata, and was developed in the second great epic, the Rāmāyana, 'story of Rāma'. In the final versions of this poem Rāma is the Avatar of Vishnu and his wife Sītā is the Avatar of his consort Lakshmī. These two figures are models of both divine and human conduct, and their love for each other is true married bliss.

[19] K. Klostermaier, *Hindu and Christian in Vrindaban*, 1969, pp. 14 f.

In the medieval devotional movements the Rāma cult developed, and Tulsī Dās made his own Hindi version of the Rāmāyana as 'the Holy Lake of the Acts of Rāma'. Here the Avatar is more like a true incarnation than in other stories, Rāma suffering 'like an ordinary man', and from his birth 'the Lord of lords became a child and began to cry'. There have been differences of opinion as to whether Tulsī Dās was a monist, a qualified non-dualist, or even a dualist. He seems closest to the position of Rāmānuja, but he was independent and his theoretical views which may appear at times to be non-dualistic were qualified by his devotional needs. He refers to the Brahman without attributes, and its unity with the soul, but his emphasis upon *bhakti* for the personal God Rāma made his mysticism unitary without being identification.[20] He tells us himself that 'all the sages whom I questioned told me that God is present in all creation; but this doctrine of the impersonal did not satisfy me; I became ever more attached to the Absolute made personal'.

Kabīr is one of the best known and most popular Indian saints and famed as both mystic and religious reformer. He is unique in being revered by Hindus and Muslims, some of his hymns being included in the scriptures of the Sikhs, and himself having a following that still claims to number over a million. He is also well known outside India, and is hailed as both a devotional poet and a teacher of non-dualistic monism. He spoke of God being present in temple and mosque, and known by the names of Allah and Rāma. But he had no time for the Avatars, in the Krishna sense, for he said that they all died, whereas only the One is eternal and has no attributes.

Kabīr uses love symbolism for his adoration of Rāma, though not in any erotic manner, rather as the longing of the soul for the Beatific Vision, the sight of the divine Beloved. The pangs of separation from God are suggested, but sensual pleasure is not regarded as adequate to indicate the union of the soul with ultimate Reality. For Kabīr Rām or Nām, the name, is a way of apprehending the divine being and finally merging into it. Rather like a Sūfī mystic Kabīr sought an identity with the divine being to such an extent that his own self would be absorbed.

[20] F. R. Allchin, *Kavitāvalī*, 1964, p. 47; W. D. P. Hill, *The Holy Lake of the Acts of Rāma*, 1952, p. 484.

Repeating 'Thou, Thou', I became Thou,
in me, no 'I' remained:
Offering myself unto Thy Name,
wherever I look, Thou art![21]

Kabīr entered into a tradition of holy men, Sants, in which
importance was placed upon the teacher, the Guru, who could be
regarded almost as God himself. The Guru emphasis continued in
the Sikh religion, from the founder Guru Nānak, down through the
nine other Gurus who succeeded him. The Gurus were taken as
models of life and devotion, each of them being virtually identified
with Nānak, and it is said of the believer that 'the Guru lives within
his Sikhs'.

The scriptures of the Sikhs, the Ādi Granth compiled in Punjabi
on the orders of the fifth Guru Arjun Dev and completed in 1604,
bring together the hymns of the first Sikh Gurus, and poems of a
number of other holy men, Hindu and Muslim, and give pride of
place to Kabīr. He is said to have met Guru Nānak, though critical
scholars doubt this, but he is held in high esteem by Sikhs.

Guru Nānak, from his own experience of the grace of God, taught
men to call upon the Name. In the Japji, the Sikh morning prayer, the
unity of God is asserted, his eternity, and his revelation to men
through the grace of the Guru. The Avatars are denied, though they
appear sometimes in later Sikh mythology. 'If he whom we call
Krishna were God, why was he subject to death?' An important
question for theology, on which there are differences of opinion. But
the ten Gurus, like ten Avatars, show the importance of a personal
side of religion.

Love imagery is used in the Sikh scriptures to describe the
approach of the worshipper to union with the Beloved. So in a hymn
attributed to Guru Nānak:

I would repeat the holy Name of the Lord;
Thus let the soul step by step
Mount the stairs to the Bridegroom
And become one with Him.[22]

[21] C. Vaudeville, *Kabīr*, 1974, p. 173.
[22] T. Singh and others, *Selections from the Sacred Writings of the Sikhs*, 1960, p. 47.

And Guru Arjun sang of 'the path to Union' in the destruction of self, and the discovery of the Lord within the soul. But this abstract statement is then enriched with the imagery of the Beloved, the lover decking himself with ornaments, the revelation of the divine Face, and the finding of the Beloved like a lost jewel.[23]

LOVE FOR ŚIVA

The worship of Śiva has existed parallel to that of Vishnu for centuries, dominating in many places, and perhaps traceable back to the cross-legged and masked 'proto-Yogi' and 'proto-Śiva' of the Indus Valley seals, some four thousand years ago. Despite his fearsome character Śiva is regarded with love, and he is held to appear in grace to his devotees. There is asceticism and eroticism in the myths of Śiva and his consort Devī, but there are no Avatars properly speaking and devotional movements and hymns are not erotic.

Kabīr had something of the spirit of a Śiva poetess of the fourteenth century, Lallā, the first poetess in the Kashmiri language and revered by Hindus and Muslims. Lallā, like Kabīr, regarded all the names of God as equal, whether Śiva, Krishna or Jina.

> May he take from me, sick woman that I am,
> the disease of the world,
> Whether He be he, or he, or he.[24]

Probably before the tenth century there was composed a notable work in praise of Śiva, the Īśvara Gītā, the Lord's Song, part of the Kūrma Purāna, and clearly inspired by the Bhagavad Gītā. This work combines philosophy from the Upanishads, theories of Yoga, Śaivite theism, and *bhakti* devotion. Many phrases are borrowed from the Bhagavad Gītā, but for the transfiguration of Krishna there is substituted Śiva in his world-shattering dance, that representation of the dancing God which appears in countless bronze and painted reproductions.

The Īśvara Gītā teaches the love of God for those who come to

---

[23] Ibid., p. 193.

[24] Lallā-Vākyāni, tr. G. Grierson and L. D. Barnett, 1920, p. 30.

him for help, 'I love those who implore me, and I love them as they implore me' (11.72). Man's love for God is itself a gift of the grace of God, 'Our faithful love is born by your grace' (5.44). There is a lower devotion which is shown by acts of worship and action without hope of reward, and a higher love which leads to mystical union. The first stage towards this is knowledge of unmanifested being, the second stage is identity with the divine essence of Brahman, but the final stage is mystical union with the supreme God, entering into his most secret body.

> Yogis who know the truth
> enter into my most secret body
> which penetrates everything,
> and they obtain imperishable union with me. (2.52)

Salvation is 'supreme union with me', Nirvāna, oneness with Brahman, isolation, which sages know. There seems an attempt at including all ways to unity, monist, Buddhist and yogic, and also an indication that all paths of salvation find their fulfilment in loving union with God.[25]

In southern India there was a great flowering of devotional literature in praise of Śiva in the Tamil Śaiva Siddhānta, and it has been claimed as one of the purest streams of monotheism in India. Twenty-eight Siddhāntas, 'texts', were said to have been inspired by Śiva himself and revealed to his devotees, and they teach salvation and union with God. In these texts God is transcendent, great and fearful, but he is also immanent in the world, creating and sustaining all things, and dissolving everything into himself at the end of each world-cycle. God resides in souls and liberates them by his power from involvement with evil.

Although there is no Avatar, there is both the divine immanence in the world and the appearance of God as Guru to his devotees. One of the most popular of the Tamil poet-mystics, Mānikka Vāchakar, composed verses that are sung daily in temples and homes throughout Tamil country. He spoke of the presence of God in all

---

[25] *L'Īśvaragītā*, tr. P. E. Dumont, 1933; and see M. Dhavamony, *Love of God according to Śaiva Siddhānta*, pp. 89 f.

lives, 'yet not confused with any of them', and he sang of the divine appearance.

> The One, the most precious,
> the Infinite, came down to earth;
> I did not despise his descent as Guru
> who appeared in grace.[26]

Imagery of love is used about Śiva; God is the lover, and his follower is a love-sick woman who is only seeking union with him, as he desires it with her. This means that although non-dualistic language is sometimes used in Śaivite writings, yet the personal God and the language of love make its goal union without identity. At the end of his important study Fr Dhavamony maintains that:

> Śaiva Siddhānta does not consider the non-dualist type of mysticism as having ultimate value in religious life, because such an experience is closed up in the unique self and is based on the false suppositions of non-dualism itself and of all that it implies. On the other hand, it proposes love of God as the key to the genuine religious experience.[27]

Śaiva Siddhānta shares with other Indian works a belief in the eternity, even divinity, of the soul. In its own nature the soul is divine in essence, but when it is fettered by ignorance and evil this is not known, and it becomes divinized only by surrender to and union with God. In this teaching, God is love and all that he does in the world has the object of leading men to union with himself in love. This is a theistic mysticism which has comparable elements with Christian mysticism.

MODERN MYSTICS

Reference has been made to the pantheistic teaching of Rāmakrishna, or more clearly of his followers, and to the more theistic doctrines of Aurobindo. Further lines of thought can be seen in modern reform movements. In the early days of the Brāhmo

[26] Dhavamony, *Love of God according to Śaiva Siddhānta*, p. 160.
[27] Ibid., p. 378.

Samāj there was a desire to return to the Vedas, beyond the idolatry and superstition of later times. Notions of Avatars were rejected and yet a personal God was sought. The patriarchal Devendranath Tagore, one of the leaders of Hindu reform (1818–1905), however, confessed his disappointment with the monism of the Upanishads and their later interpretation by Śankara.

> Shankarâchârya has turned India's head by preaching the doctrine of Monism; the identity of God and man. Following his teachings, both ascetics and men of the world are repeating this senseless formula, 'I am that Supreme Deity'.[28]

He declared that he wanted to worship God, but if worshipper and the object of worship became one then there could be no worship. Hence both Upanishads and Śankara had failed, and what was needed was a religion of the pure heart in which God would be seen by worship and meditation.

Such teachings were continued by the even more famous son, Rabindranath Tagore. He was better known in the early decades of this century than now, and celebrations of his birth concentrated upon his nationalist writings, now very tame, rather than upon his outstanding poetry. Yet Tagore made a great impact, was supported by W. B. Yeats and others, and received the Nobel prize for literature in 1913. Tagore's perhaps over-romantic English writings have been criticized, and there may have been some decline in his later works, but he is claimed as supreme in Bengali and his poems and plays are popular all over India.

In Gitanjali, 'song offerings', his best English collection of poems and constantly reprinted, Tagore reveals a religious spirit of a high order. It has been said that he was feeling after the Christian God of love, but there are many indications of the Indian setting. God is the divine flute-player, like Krishna, yet he is also breaking stones in the dust outside the temple, and his feet rest 'among the poorest and lowliest, and lost'. The deity is also Mother, like Kālī, or a great king, like Śiva, who comes down from his throne to stop at our cottage door.

[28] *The Autobiography of Maharshi Devendranath Tagore*, 1915, pp. 199, 72, 161.

The principal note of Tagore is love, and in this he shows himself a theistic mystic, for it is the purest love which recognizes the divine initiative and the distinction between God and man that is needed for communion.

> Let only that little be left of my will
> whereby I may feel thee on every side,
> and come to thee in everything,
> and offer to thee my love every moment.[29]

Such modern Indian mystics recognize the importance of the world; God is not in the dark corner of a temple with doors all shut. There may be influences from other religious traditions here, but there is also a return to the practical concerns of the Bhagavad Gītā with its scorn for the hypocritical ascetic. Further, alongside the passionate devotions of medieval and other periods, there flourished great material civilizations whose inspiration was both this-worldly and other worldly. In many different ways, the mystical search for unity found the divine Being in all forms of life.

[29] R. Tagore, *Gitanjali*, 1913, 34.

Chapter 10

BIBLE AND CABBALAH

'Pre-Christian Judaism', asserted R. C. Zaehner, 'is not only un-mystical, it is anti-mystical ... exclusively obsessed by the transcendent holiness of God and man's nothingness in face of him.' God is a great and terrifying mystery in the Bible, and 'not even in the Qur'ān does this *mysterium tremendum* make itself so tremendously felt'. Though the edge is taken off this statement when a few pages later this author says of the Qur'ān, 'Not even in the Old Testament do you have such an over-mastering insight into Omnipotence.'[1]

The notion that the Old Testament is 'exclusively obsessed' with the transcendence of God arises from the elementary mistake of considering it as a single and homogeneous book, instead of an anthology which includes many points of view, from myth to law, from prophecy to wisdom, and from formal to personal religion. Of course the transcendence of God is affirmed, and he is 'high and lifted up', but that man is 'nothing' is nowhere stated. When Abraham was reported to have said that he was 'dust and ashes' it was when he was communing personally with the Lord as a friend. It is even exceptional to find a verse which states that a man was 'shaped in iniquity and conceived in sin', for this is a personal statement and the later doctrine of original sin is a Christian notion which has little support in the Old Testament.

Some modern writers, particularly followers of Karl Barth, speak of the great 'gulf' between man and God who is the 'Wholly Other',

[1] R. C. Zaehner, *At Sundry Times*, 1958, pp. 15, 27, 171.

MYSTICISM IN THE WORLD'S RELIGIONS

and it is assumed that such ideas are constant biblical themes. But the only reference to such a gulf in the Bible comes in the New Testament parable of Dives and Lazarus, where it refers to a gulf between heaven and hell. Zaehner in his last book carried his attack further against 'the savage Lord of Armies [who] rages in the horror of the storm'.[2] He seemed to have an animus against Yahweh, if one may use this approximation to the unknown Name, the mysterious if not the mystical, and it is strange that he did not show the same revulsion for the much more terrifying Śiva of Indian mysticism, who haunts cemeteries, feeds on flesh, dances to destroy the world in fire, but also appears to his devotees in love.

The interpretation of the Old Testament as 'a bloody book' with a 'savage God' stresses the dark side at the expense of the light, and both are there; it is also blind to the development both of doctrine and morality in the Bible, where the crudity and harshness of Joshua and Jehu, for example, are tempered and challenged by Hosea and Deutero-Isaiah. Both Dietrich Bonhoeffer and Zaehner insisted that it is 'one and the same God' in Old and New Testaments, and that it is 'very naïve' to speak of the former as an earlier stage of religion.[3] But in fact it was naïve of these scholars not to recognize the actual historical earlier stage of the Old Testament, and to ignore the results of over a century of biblical research which has demolished the notion of 'one Book'. Of course God is always the same, he is unchangeable, but it is elementary to state that men's understanding of God differs greatly in successive ages, and that men may learn from the past and progress to a better understanding of God. When Hosea condemned 'the blood of Jezreel upon the house of Jehu' he was expressing revulsion against the violence even of Jehu's religious reform. And Jesus himself affirmed, 'It was said, An eye for an eye, and a tooth for a tooth: but I say unto you, Resist not him that is evil.'

Rabbi Barnett Joseph, in a lecture on *Aspects of Jewish Mysticism*,[4] declared that 'the Bible is the world's greatest classic of mysticism'. This follows a dictionary definition of a mystic as 'one

[2] R. C. Zaehner, *Our Savage God*, pp. 261 f.
[3] Ibid., p. 220.
[4] Published in *Common Ground*, Autumn 1972.

who seeks or attains direct intercourse with God in elevated religious feeling or ecstasy'. In various books of the Bible examples are found of forms of mystical experience, devotional, speculative and practical. From the very first page of the Torah there is the Spirit of God hovering over the waters of chaos, and then man is made in the image of the Creator. Indeed God breathes into man the breath of life, which is the Holy Spirit, and must be by definition immortal. It would appear that the living soul in man is God himself, and there could hardly be a closer union. Then at death, according to Ecclesiastes, 'The spirit returns to God who gave it.'

It would be tedious to list the references in the Old Testament to the presence and nearness of God. Isaiah not only spoke of God as high and lifted up, transcendent, but also 'with him that is of a contrite and humble spirit', immanent. The Psalmists often felt the presence of God, as in Psalm 139, which asks, 'Whither shall I go from thy spirit, or whither shall I flee from thy presence?' Thomas Aquinas, who spoke of mysticism as the knowledge of God through experience, constantly used the words of the Psalmist, 'Oh taste and see that the Lord is good'. To taste and see is experiential, and the mystical outlook is determined by experience of God. 'To walk humbly with your God' (Micah 6.8) was regarded as the true demand of the divine.

There are many visions recounted in the Bible, and they need not be dismissed as unmystical out of hand since we shall argue later that visions are more significant and common than is sometimes thought. Yet although the Bible is often thought to be crude and anthropomorphic it shows a proper reserve in descriptions of visions of God. Isaiah claimed that he saw the Lord but never attempted to describe him, nor did Moses or Job in their divine experiences. It may be said that visions do not give the experience of mystical unity,[5] but they do reveal many different experiences of God in men separated by character and time.

Many expressions are used about God in the Old Testament, such as father, friend, shepherd and guide, but especially interesting are similes of marriage, which is the fullest union. The Old Testament begins with the separation of Eve from Adam, and the New

[5] R. C. Zaehner, *At Sundry Times*, p. 171.

113

Testament ends with the sacred divine marriage, the espousals of the new Jerusalem, 'made ready as a bride adorned for her husband . . . the bride, the wife of the Lamb'.

The Song of Songs is the *locus classicus* of mystical imagery for Judaism and Christianity, and whatever its original purpose it became both to Israel and the Church, by admission into their canon, the source of statements about the love of God and his union with his people. 'The graces of the church', says the heading in the Authorised Version to the passage which speaks of 'thy two breasts are like two young roes that are twins, which feed among the lilies', an erotic passage that may be compared with Krishna's praises of Rādhā. Other passages from this book are used in the offices of the Blessed Virgin Mary, and of course these are adaptations beyond what the original text implied. But the most striking example in the Old Testament itself of the divine marriage, which is the closest form of unity, comes in the prophecy of Hosea. Here the prophet marries a prostitute, 'even as the Lord loves the children of Israel', and when she goes astray it is as 'the land commits great whoredom, departing from the Lord'. Yet he is her husband and she is his wife, and when she returns to him 'You will call me My Husband (Ishi) and no more My Master' (Baali; Hosea 2.16). So much for 'the savage God', for 'I will not return to destroy Ephraim, for I am God, and not man' (11.9). It is this God who takes men in his arms, heals them, and 'draws them with cords of a man, with bonds of love'. In him 'the fatherless finds mercy', for 'I will heal their backsliding, I will love them freely'.

DEVELOPING JUDAISM

Judaism strictly refers to the descendants of Judah and so, as Muhammad saw, 'Abraham was not a Jew' since he was Judah's great-grandfather. But after the fall of the kingdom of Judah in 586, the term Judaism comes to be applied to the period of the Exile in Babylon, and later and more particularly from the Maccabean period and the Christian era. After the Old Testament the performance of ritual as long as the Temple stood at Jerusalem, and the preoccupation of the rabbis with interpretations of the Law, may

BIBLE AND CABBALAH

both be regarded as quenching the spirit of prophetic fervour or mystical communion. But just as excavations of ancient synagogues have sometimes shown their decorations to be far more lavish than might have been expected from the iconoclastic decrees of ancient time, so the living religion may have been much richer than the rather cold surviving documents suggest.

The Talmud, which became the great body of interpretation and expansion of traditional doctrine, affirms both the transcendence and the immanence of God. A common term for God is 'the Place', since 'He is the place of the universe', though it is carefully added that 'the universe is not his place'. Especially is the Shechinah, the 'dwelling', the presence and the light of God, as light diffuses itself throughout the world. The Shechinah was manifested in the Tabernacle and Temple, since God both fills the worlds and can restrict himself into a small space. The Shechinah is in the midst of those who study the Torah, and shares in human sorrows.[6]

The Talmud teaches both that God is a unity and that he has no bodily form, yet rather surprisingly it uses language about God which is both anthropomorphic and expressive of the divine nearness to man. God is said to wear phylacteries and a prayer shawl to study the Torah and pray. He arranged the marriage of Adam and Eve, plaiting the bride's hair and acting as groomsman. He visits the sick, weeps over his failing creatures and buries the dead.[7]

The Bible had said not only that man is made in the image of God, but 'You are gods, and all of you sons of the Most High' (Psalm 72.6), and the Talmud repeats this while maintaining that man is a creature with a mortal body. Created in the divine image, by the special love of God, one man is equal to all the rest of creation. The purpose of human life, as of the whole world, is to glorify God. It has often been noted that Hebrew religion, from the Bible onwards, is life-affirming, since God created the world and 'saw that it was good'. Hence asceticism and celibacy are rare, and marriage is the norm even for priests and rabbis. But we are trying to show that it is a fallacy to regard mysticism as necessarily linked with world-denial, and it has been seen that the Chinese Taoists sought for mystical union by the affirmation of nature and the world.

[6] See A. Cohen, *Everyman's Talmud*, 1949 edn, pp. 8, 42 f.   [7] Ibid., p. 7.

115

The study of the Torah was the paramount duty of Jews since it was the guide to life and the knowledge of God. But while meticulous study of text and commentary, and provision for every circumstance of life, may have been pedestrian, mystical interpretations developed. The Shechinah abides among ten people who meet together to study the Torah, since it had been said that 'God stands in the congregation of the godly' (Psalm 82.1). Many passages were given deeper meanings, and notable are teachings of the Talmud which developed the first chapter of Genesis and spoke of saints 'who entered the Garden', involving an ascension into the invisible world and intimate communion with the divine.

CABBALISM AND HASIDISM

Gershom Scholem, in his great work on *Major Trends in Jewish Mysticism*, says very little of the Bible and not much of the Talmud, and concentrates on the later Cabbalism and Hasidism. Yet this might appear to support those who claim that Judaism only became mystical when influenced by Neoplatonism and Islamic Sufism, and so it has been important to stress the biblical and Talmudic roots of Jewish mysticism. Passages in the Bible such as the accounts of creation in Genesis, and visions like those of Isaiah in the temple and Ezekiel seeing cherubim and the divine chariot, not only raised questions about the divine nature and activity but provided material for the speculations of later centuries. There are mystical discussions in the Talmud on the Work of Creation and the Divine Chariot which gave rise to ascetic disciplines and trances in order to attain to heavenly ascents and descents.[8]

In medieval times there were schools of practical and speculative mysticism which developed into the Cabbalah (Kabbalah, 'tradition'). Both kinds were concerned with the divine nature, but the Provençal-Spanish school of Isaac the Blind and Moses de Leon in the twelfth and thirteenth centuries exercised the most profound influence, which has lasted to this day. The long and complex work called the Zohar, 'Splendour', provided an exposition of mystical speculation. God is here described as En Sof, the endless and infinite

[8] See I. Epstein, *Judaism*, 1959, pp. 224 f.

and all. 'For all things are in him and he is in all things: he is both manifest and concealed. Manifest in order to uphold the whole, and concealed for he is found nowhere.'[9] God projected from himself ten Sefiroth, channels of light (perhaps from *sappir*, sapphire rays), by which the divine existence became perceptible and comprehensible. The last of the Sefiroth is the Shechinah, 'indwelling', the presence of God in individuals, communities and places.

The unity of God and the world was believed to have been originally complete, in the harmony of En Sof and the Shechinah, but when evil appeared there was disorder and the Shechinah is now in exile, appearing only in isolated persons and places. The goal of existence, therefore, is the restoration of the original unity, through moral perfection and communion with God. Every individual must aim at this divine unity, but it is particularly communal, and when the Messiah comes and the Temple rises again then the Shechinah will be reunited with God and all things will return to the original harmony.

The Zohar teaches that love is the secret of the divine unity, and in both moral and devotional work 'Love unites the highest and lowest stages and lifts everything to the stage where all must be one.'[10] With the Shechinah there is a divine marriage, a 'sacred union' of king and queen. Adam and Eve also symbolize union, 'to embrace, like us', the four quarters of the world, and man may often be in communion with the divine. For when the Bible said that Abraham continued his 'journeys', the plural indicated the divine presence with him, the 'heavenly mate' which provides a constant union.

The love of God is found in many verses of the Zohar in expositions of biblical texts, for when 'Jacob kisses Rachel' (Gen. 29.11) it is the Lord who embraces each holy soul, fondling her and presenting gifts. There is a palace of love where every beloved soul enters to receive the divine kisses. Indeed God himself is pierced with shafts of heavenly love in his heart from the objects of his desire. Knowledge itself, remarks Scholem, means the realization of union, and 'this received a sublime erotic quality' which is often stressed in Cabbalistic works.[11]

[9] *Zohar*, E.T. 1931–4, III, 288a.   [10] *Zohar*, II, 216a.
[11] G. G. Scholem, *Major Trends in Jewish Mysticism*, 1955, pp. 227, 235.

The development and extension of Cabbalism were so vast that interested readers must be referred to general works, like that of Epstein, or specialist studies, such as that of Scholem. Cabbalism played a great role in the struggles of medieval Jewry and more even than the Bible it gave them a sense of spiritual power in times of material and physical distress. Yet while Cabbalistic thought and speculative doctrines spread widely throughout the Middle Ages, it was only from the eighteenth century that the masses in Judaism came under the direct influence of Cabbalism through the Hasidic movement.

Hasidists (Chassidists), 'pious', appeared at different times during the course of Jewish history, but there was a great revival in the mystical fervour of the eighteenth century which still has thousands of followers. The Hasidic masters used Cabbalistic ideas and adapted them to their own mystical expressions. Baal Shem Tov, the founder of modern Hasidism, has sometimes been called a pantheist, but he was rather panentheist, seeing all things in God, but not identifying God with the world in Indian pantheistic or monistic fashion. Since 'there is no place empty of God', the divine being may be found in ordinary things of everyday life, rather than in the practice of asceticism. Yet worldly things are only a means for the apprehension of God, and the ultimate aim is the 'annihilation of self' and rising through contemplation to the all that is in God.[12]

Hasidism, teaches methods of contemplation, the general method being to dwell on the immanence of God in everything, and the second to reflect in detail on the divine presence in particular creatures. The Zaddik, 'righteous', sought constantly to please the One and Unique by apprehending the divine unity and the unification of all in him. It all comes to one thing, 'the comprehension of the simple unity alone . . . in which man binds his soul to His true essence, blessed be He, alone'.[13]

The Hasidic movement has been popularized for the modern world by Martin Buber, especially in his little book *I and Thou*, a title rather too formal and liturgical in English, and perhaps better rendered in the intimacy of colloquialism as *You and Me*. Buber

[12] L. Jacobs, *Hasidic Prayer*, 1972, pp. 9 f.
[13] Ibid., p. 92.

holds that 'the one primary word is the combination I-Thou. The other primary word is the combination I-It', and the difference between relations with persons and things is fundamental. Since true relationships are in meeting, knowledge of God is meeting him in the world and beyond it. 'Of course God is the "wholly Other"; but He is also the wholly Same, the wholly Present. Of course He is the *Mysterium Tremendum* that appears and overthrows; but He is also the mystery of the self-evident, nearer to me than my I.'[14]

Buber has maintained that mystical unity does not mean identity with God. In experience we may feel an undivided unity, but he calls this 'an original pre-biographical unity'. It is very easy, especially in a pantheistic environment, to mistake this basic unity in one's own soul for identity with the divine Being, but the monotheistic religions generally guide their followers away from this seduction. Buber contradicts those who maintain that the I and Thou are superficial, and that deep down there is only one primal being without any relationships. Such monism need not even envisage a divine being and consists simply in saying that the existent exists.[15]

Scholem writes in a similar manner:

It is only in extremely rare cases that ecstasy signifies actual union with God, in which the human individuality abandons itself to the rapture of complete submersion in the divine stream. Even in this ecstatic frame of mind, the Jewish mystic almost invariably retains a sense of the distance between the Creator and His creature. The latter is joined to the former, and the point where the two meet is of the greatest interest to the mystic, but he does not regard it as constituting anything so extravagant as identity of Creator and creature.[16]

Here is the true distinction, between communion and union on the one hand, and identity on the other. Identification with God in the sense of 'Thou art That', or 'I am God', is rejected not only by Jewish mystics but by nearly all Christian mystics, by orthodox Sufis, and by monotheistic Hindus going back to Rāmānuja and the Bhagavad

---

[14] Martin Buber, *I and Thou*. E.T. 1937, p. 79.

[15] Martin Buber, *Between Man and Man*. E.T. 1947, pp. 24 f.

[16] G. G. Scholem, *Major Trends in Jewish Mysticism*, pp. 122 f.

Gītā. This is the watershed in mysticism, not between prophecy and wisdom, or Semitic and Indian, but between theism and monism, between communion and identity.

Chapter 11

MUHAMMAD AND THE SUFIS

THE EXPERIENCES OF MUHAMMAD

'In Islam', it has been said, 'we cannot help feeling that Sufism is so radical a distortion of the orthodox doctrine as to constitute almost a separate religion.' And this is held to be so because, like the Old Testament, the Qur'ān is supposed to emphasize 'overwhelmingly the complete otherness of God'.[1]

The Qur'ān is more of a unity than the Old Testament, but as religion rather than systematic theology it has varied teachings about God. The Qur'ān has been closely linked with one man, the Prophet Muhammad, but was he as unmystical as the above quotation suggests? No great religious figure has been so maligned as Muhammad. Attacked in the past as a heretic, an imposter, or a sensualist, it is still possible to find him referred to in otherwise academic writings as 'the false prophet'. A modern German writer accuses Muhammad of sensuality, surrounding himself with young women. This man was not married till he was twenty-five years of age, then he and his wife lived in happiness and fidelity for twenty-four years, until her death when he was forty-nine. Only between the age of fifty and his death at sixty-two did Muhammad take other wives, only one of whom was a virgin, and most of them were taken for dynastic and political reasons. Certainly the Prophet's record was much better than that head of the Church of England, Henry VIII.

Muhammad was an able administrator, a careful politician and a

---

[1] R. C. Zaehner, *Hindu and Muslim Mysticism*, 1960, pp. 2 f.

121

brave soldier, but he was primarily and always a prophet and a man of God. Yet can he in any way be claimed as a mystic? Or were his prophecy and experience so different from mysticism as to mark a great divide between prophecy and wisdom? That many Muslims have claimed Muhammad as a mystic is an important fact, which should be taken into account, even though Western critics have tended to regard this as a later production of the religious consciousness, which insisted on attributing all virtues and saintliness to the Prophet.

Muhammad certainly had disturbing religious experiences, and whether they can be interpreted as mystical depends partly upon whether we allow ourselves to be persuaded by some writers into excluding all visions and dreams from mysticism, or whether with other scholars we regard them as common in mystical experience.

The standard biography of the Prophet, compiled about a hundred years after his death, gives several traditional versions of his religious experiences and allows of different interpretations. Muhammad was forty years old when 'God sent him in compassion to mankind'. His youngest wife later said that God had made him love solitude, and he liked nothing better than to be alone. He went into the desert, like Elijah and Jesus, and the early Christian monks. Then the signs of prophecy were given to him, being called 'true visions . . . shown to him in his sleep'. As he went to his solitary vigils Muhammad heard the stones and trees salute him as 'the Apostle of God', though when he looked round he could 'see nothing but trees and stones'. He ascended Mount Hira near Mecca every year for a month to practise devotion, and he would give food to the poor who came to him. At the end of the month he walked seven times round the sacred shrine of the Ka'ba in Mecca before returning to his own house.[2]

Finally Muhammad was asleep in a cave on Mount Hira when the angel Gabriel brought him the command of God. On one occasion he saw a colossal figure with feet astride the horizon, and wherever he looked there was this figure. Then again Gabriel came and drew near with a coverlet of brocade whereon was some writing, and said 'Read'. He pressed Muhammad with it tightly so that he thought it

[2] *The Life of Muhammad*, tr. A. Guillaume, 1955, pp. 104 f.

was death, and said 'Read'. Muhammad asked, 'What shall I read?',
and he recited chapter 96 of the Qur'ān, traditionally the first to be
revealed,

> Read, in the name of thy Lord who created,
> created man of blood coagulated.

The Qur'ān itself is a century earlier, always accepted as uttered
through Muhammad and considered by some Western scholars as
written by him. It is not an autobiography, but its occasional glimpses
of the Prophet's religious experiences are sharp and impressive.
About these two visions it says of the celestial figure:

> He stood upright on the high horizon,
> then he came near and let himself down
> until he was two bow-lengths near or almost,
> and he told his servant what he told him . . .
> He saw him again at a second descent,
> by the plum-tree at the boundary . . .
> when the tree was strangely enveloped.
> the eye did not turn aside or pass its limits,
> and truly he saw one of the greatest signs of his Lord.[3]

There is no suggestion in the Qur'ān that this celestial figure was
Gabriel, and critical scholars like Bell and Watt consider that 'it was
God' that Muhammad thought he had seen. If this is so then God
was not excessively transcendent in the Qur'ān.

Another possible experience, which has only a tantalizing
reference in the Qur'ān, was made much of in later mystical teaching.
This was the supposed Night Journey of the Prophet to Jerusalem,
and his Ascension from thence to heaven. The biographer reports
that 'the apostle's body remained where it was but God removed his
spirit by night'. Later legend, cherished to this day, saw the Prophet
riding on a winged mule and flying up to the seventh heaven, and for
mystics this symbolized the soul's ascent through successive circles
up to God. But in the Qur'ān there is only a brief and enigmatic
statement: 'Glory to him who travelled with his servant by night from
the Holy Mosque to the Farther Mosque', and it would be unwise to
read a mystical meaning into this verse alone.[4]

[3] 53.6–18.   [4] 17.1.

More significant are the 'Mantle' verses of two chapters of the Qur'ān:

> O you who are wrapped in garments
> watch almost the whole night,
> or half the night, a little less or more . . .
>
> O you who are wrapped in your mantle,
> Arise and warn!
> Magnify your Lord, purify your garments . . .
> wait patiently for your Lord.[5]

The mantle (*dathār*) was a sort of outer garment, and it is said that the Prophet covered himself with a mantle when the revelation came to him. Some modern commentators give the ordinary interpretation that after his first experience Muhammad was cold and was ordered to wrap himself up in his clothes. But Kenneth Cragg says that 'there is nothing more intimately personal than attire', and the reference to the robe could make 'a focal point of self-confrontation'. But he admits that mantles have been, since Elijah at least, symbols of prophetic authority and there are traces of similar ideas among Arabian soothsayers.[6]

In his book, *The Mystical Elements in Muhammad*, J. C. Archer suggests that the mantle was used by Muhammad as part of a deliberate technique to induce a mystical state. It was not a robe, but a 'tent' thrown over the head, to isolate the wearer from sense-distraction and enable him to concentrate his mind. Rather like a Yogi, the Prophet would then achieve a state of trance or separation from the physical world, leading to self-control and union with God.

Cragg rejects the notion of deliberately induced experiences in Muhammad, and Watt says that the early messages clearly came unexpectedly, though no doubt with time Muhammad may have developed some method of 'listening' while he slowly recited the Qur'ān at night.[7] That the Prophet had unusual experiences is generally admitted, despite the tendency of some modern inter-

---

[5] 73.1–3; 74.1–7.
[6] K. Cragg, *The Event of the Qur'ān*, 1971, p. 34.
[7] W. M. Watt, *Muhammad at Mecca*, 1953, pp. 52 f.

preters to reduce everything to the ordinary and dull. Though he was accused of being mad or possessed, Muhammad resisted such explanations of the objective visions he had received:

Your companion is not mad,
he saw him on the clear horizon.[8]

Indeed Muhammad's revulsion from the antics of the ecstatics was so profound that it urged him to suicide. 'None of God's creatures was more hateful to me than an ecstatic poet or a man possessed . . . I will go to the top of the mountain and throw myself down that I may kill myself and gain rest.' But then the figure appeared astride the horizon and called him the Apostle of God.[9]

The words that came to Muhammad were sometimes called 'suggestions' or 'promptings', that is to say, divine revelation. Tradition reported that sometimes he heard the words 'like the reverberation of a bell'. He would stream with perspiration even on a cold day, and pain gripped him, but when the distress passed away he laughed. Sometimes he saw an angel in the form of a man, but at other times the words simply appeared in his heart. God is also said to have spoken to Muhammad 'from behind a veil', which suggests that in such cases there was no vision but what has been called an 'interior locution'. Or perhaps it was an 'exterior locution' in that the Prophet heard voices, like Joan of Arc, which seemed to come from outside himself.

Critics of Islam have spoken of Muhammad as a 'pathological case' or 'a diseased genius', and his experiences have been explained away in terms of hypnosis and autosuggestion. One of the commonest accusations has been epilepsy, which has been applied to other great men from St Paul to Luther and Napoleon. The symptoms of epilepsy are not identical with those described for Muhammad's trances, there was no physical or mental degeneration, and he went on to become a great leader, ruler, soldier and teacher, who died in the full possession of his faculties.

Watt, in his perceptive study of Muhammad's prophetic consciousness,[10] points out that such criticisms are not only false but

[8] 81.23–4.   [9] *The Life of Muhammad*, tr. A. Guillaume, p. 106.
[10] W. M. Watt, *Muhammad at Mecca*, pp. 52 ff.

irrelevant. To suggest that Muhammad's voices and visions were hallucinations is to make serious theological judgements, which could be applied equally to many Christian mystics, from St Paul onwards. Whether the voices were exterior or interior does not affect their validity or meaning.

Tor Andrae, in *The Psychology of Mysticism*, distinguishes two types of inspiration, the auditory and the visual. He says that Muhammad apparently belonged to the auditory type (though he also saw visions) because his revelations were dictated to him by a voice. Andrae finds a proof of the genuineness of inspiration in a verse that speaks of dictating the Qur'ān (75.16), since many inspired persons find that any trace of personal initiative hampers the flow of inspiration.

Not only visions and voices but the contents of the message are important for establishing the claim that Muhammad had mystical feelings of the immanence of God as well as his transcendence. The basic teaching is expressed in the Witness or Testimony: 'There is no god' (small g) 'but God' (capital). This means that God is the only real deity, and God (Allāh), like Yahweh, is a personal name which has no plural. From epithets applied to him it is clear that God is regarded as eternal, omnipotent, omniscient, and the only reality. Later Sufis developed this to mean that only God exists, and that men are one with or identical with him.

The most commonly recited attributes of God in the Qur'ān are in the Bismillah, 'in the name of God', which heads every chapter but one: 'In the name of God, the Compassionate, the Merciful', or the Compassionate Compassionator. Closely akin to this are the Most Beautiful Names, a phrase occurring several times in the Qur'ān, many of which are used to fit in with the rhymes of the verses. This recitation of the divine attributes became popular in devotion, and mystical groups tell over the names on prayer beads and sway to and fro while chanting them. There are said to be Ninety-nine Beautiful Names, while the hundredth remains unknown, except perhaps to saints, like the Hebrew unutterable name.

In relationship to mankind the Qur'ān sees God not only as Compassionate but as working in a personal providence. One long chapter (55) has a constant refrain telling of the benefits of the Lord, and other verses speak of providence even to animals. Some of the most moving verses reflect personal experience. Muhammad had an unhappy childhood; his father died before he was born, his mother when he was six, and his grandfather when he was eight, leaving him in the care of an uncle with a large family. So the Qur'ān declares:

> Did he not find you an orphan and give you shelter?
> Did he not find you wandering and guide you?
> Did he not find you poor and enrich you?[11]

The Qur'ān speaks not only of the greatness of God above the world, and his clear personality, but of his working in the world, 'which amounts to immanence', says the *Encyclopaedia of Islam*. In addition to many verses which declare the divine activity among men, others speak of God's nearness and presence:

> We have created man, and we know
> what his soul whispers within him,
> for we are nearer to him than his jugular vein.[12]

This verse has often been interpreted mystically, and another recalls the immanence of the Gospel:

> There is not a private meeting of three
> but God is a fourth in it,
> nor of five but he is a sixth,
> nor of a lower number than that, nor a higher,
> but he is with them wherever they may be.[13]

Clearly Muhammad was impressed by the term 'the Face of God', which he often uses, as thus:

> To God belong the East and the West,
> whichever way you turn
> the Face of God is there.[14]

The Qur'ān may not be systematic but it is theistic in the highest degree and is theocentric. It has been said that Muhammad was 'God-intoxicated', a description used of other mystics like Jacob Boehme and William Blake. Unless mysticism is to be restricted to

[11] 93.6–8.   [12] 50.15.   [13] 58.8.   [14] 2.109.

pantheism, then both by his religious experiences and by his teaching Muhammad qualifies as a mystic. The fact that he was also eminently sane, a skilful religious reformer and an astute politician shows that he had practical qualities like other mystics.

For Muhammad God was the sole Creator, the only self-existent Being. It has been estimated that he would have said, without hesitation, that there was a time when nothing existed but God. Whether he would have gone further and concluded, like some Sufi mystics, that there will come a time again when nothing will exist but God cannot be stated with certainty. The essential non-existence of everything except God was later developed by theologians into an absoluteness that was extreme Deism. The Sufi mystics, on the contrary, took the other road of finding that nothing existed but God, and for some of them the world became merged into God, since he was the All, and they arrived at a virtual pantheism or monism. Muhammad held neither of these views, but the richness and variety of his teaching allowed for their development.

SUFISM

Whether Muhammad used his mantle deliberately to concentrate his mind and free it from sense distractions, as a yogi practises stillness, and as later Islamic mystics induced states of trance, may be debated. Kenneth Cragg sees the attraction of claiming that elements of later Islamic practice had their origin in the Prophet, but feels that it seems remote, 'with its Persian and Indian overtones, from the rugged native Semitic genius that speaks in the Qur'ān'. On the other hand he recognizes in another work, and in a chapter entitled 'Desiring the face of God', the value of modern studies which see Muslim theology as a mystical structure derived from the Qur'ān, and the words of the sacred book as providing the vocabulary of mysticism.[15]

Such a study was particularly the work of the great Louis Massignon, who returned to faith through his research into Sufism. Massignon combated the notion that Islamic Sufism was a foreign

[15] K. Cragg, *The Event of the Qur'ān*, pp. 34 f.; *The Mind of the Qur'ān*, 1973, p. 163.

growth, a distortion of the original monotheism, a separate religion, an importation of Indian ideas into the unmystical atmosphere of Semitic religion. He wrote:

> It is impossible to take literally the too widespread theory of the pro-Aryans . . . and the anti-Semites . . . who declare the absolute *inaptitude* of the Semites for art and science in general, and conclude with the 'aryan' origin of mysticism in the so-called Semitic religions . . . Shi'ism, which has been presented as a specifically 'Persian' Islamic heresy, was propagated in Persia by colonizers of pure Arab race . . . and the lists which have been drawn up of great Muslim thinkers 'of Persian origin' . . . are simply misleading, for the majority only thought and wrote in Arabic.[16]

Massignon went on to study the mystical tendencies in the inner life of Muhammad and themes of mystical meditation in the Qur'ān, while seeking to distinguish them from later interpretation and expansion. He questioned the opinion of Ghazālī the great Persian scholastic theologian, 1058–1111 (see p. 137 below) that Muhammad from the beginning was 'a passionate lover of God', wandering in the solitudes of Mount Hira drunk with desire for union. But Massignon refused to deny, as many orientalists have done, Muhammad's sincere and lasting devotion, marked by severe discipline, with frequent special prayers after midnight. The diversity of mystical meditations on the inner life of Muhammad shows how complex the question remains.[17]

Islamic mysticism developed from those earliest days and although it came to be called Sufism that term must be understood in a wide manner. Another great authority, J. S. Trimingham, states: 'I define the word *sūfī* in wide terms by applying it to anyone who believes that it is possible to have direct experience of God and who is prepared to go out of his way to put himself in a state whereby he may be enabled to do this,' because this has proved 'the only possible way to embrace all the varieties of people involved in the orders'.[18]

[16] L. Massignon, *Essai sur les Origines du Lexique technique de la Mystique Musulmane*, 1954, p. 64.
[17] Ibid., pp. 143 f. [18] J. S. Trimingham, *The Sufi Orders in Islam*, 1971, pp. 1 f.

Sufism, then, includes all those tendencies in Islam which seek the direct communion of God and man. It is spiritual experience which claims a knowledge of reality.

The word *sūfī*, it is well known, was first given to Muslim ascetics who wore simple clothes of wool (*sūf*), like Christian ascetics who needed simple but warm garments for their solitary vigils in desert places. There was undoubtedly some Christian influence, and Muhammad himself spoke appreciatively of Christian monks whose hermitages shone as lights in the desert. In the early centuries Islamic mystics frequented Christian monasteries and studied their devotional literature. But Sufism was a natural development within Islam, both as a reaction against the worldliness resulting from the success of the Arab armies, and as a search for a more pure and inward religion. It owed little to non-Islamic sources and developed its own lines of thought and action. Even when later there were formulated elaborate systems which developed ideas from gnosticism and Neoplatonism, the Sufis regarded these as truly Islamic, expressing the inner mystery of the Qur'ān.

Sufis themselves have defined their practice in different ways, many of them have not worn wool, and they often refer to themselves as the 'poor', like the 'poor in spirit' of the Gospel, and expressed by the Arabic *faqīr* and Persian *darvīsh*. Sufism is not basically a system of ideas but, like other devotional movements, including Christianity and Buddhism, it is a 'Way', a Way of purification. A Sufi, by mental and spiritual discipline, like a yogi but in a quite different context, sought an experience of God in an emotional or contemplative mysticism. Round leading mystics there gathered groups of disciples, and the many 'orders' of Islamic mystics came to be known from the 'Way' (*tarīqa*) which they followed. The early teachers sought to experience rather than teach, to guide the seeker into valuable techniques of meditation, but much became formalized with time.

Mystical exercises and retreats were emphasized, as means to spiritual progress. Repetitions of litanies (*dhikr*), especially on the Ninety-nine Beautiful Names of God, aided by prayer beads, helped both to concentrate the mind and to produce an emotional state by swaying and chanting. Music, banned from the mosque, came into its own in mystical devotions. Dervish dances probably had their roots in pre-Islamic ecstatic dances, but as organized by the Persian Rūmī the 'whirling dervishes' gyrate round their sheikh in a representation of the planets circling the sun. They are called 'lovers of God' and the sheikh is the 'ambassador of God, the cypress of the garden of the Prophet, the spring of the world of knowledge, the exalted rose, the physician of hearts'. The dervishes whirl on their own axes and also in orbit, reciting inwardly the name of God: Allāh, Al-lāh, Al-lāh. With closed eyes they whirl, to the music of flutes, drums and strings, seeking union with the divine, till they cease and return to stillness. In today's performances it is decorous, but old prints show the dervishes collapsing in ecstasy and crying out in various tongues.

All of this was alarming to the orthodox, as to the worldly and sceptical, and Sufis were often persecuted. One of the principal reasons for the disfavour in which they were often held was the claim to direct experience of God, which meant by-passing established authority if not official religion itself. It was the age-old challenge of experience to orthodoxy. The legalists, who dominated so much of Islamic life, always opposed Sufism because it claimed a knowledge of God distinct from codified religion. The antagonism was not lessened by some Sufis who were extreme in both faith and practice, though others sought to keep doctrine within the bounds of Islamic orthodoxy. In modern times Sufi orders have been attacked for superstition and they have been banned in the secular state of Turkey, though the dervishes survive there and other movements, like the Nurculars, children of light, survive under a different name.

Some writers deny the existence of mysticism in the earliest years of Islam because of their 'great gulf' theory between God and man, but we have seen that this must be questioned in the Qur'ān as in the Bible. Certainly as Sufism developed any separation of God and man was overcome, in two principal ways.

The first was by teaching the love of God. Whether the Qur'ān taught the love of God has been questioned, and some theologians claimed that since there can only be love between like and like there can be no love of God and the Qur'ān simply means obedience by love. But the mystic Dhū'l-Nūn of Egypt spoke not only of love but of passionate longing as the means of journeying to God, though he preferred to speak of the vision of God rather than union with him, and he regarded love as the gift of divine grace to special souls chosen by God before the world. Some time before him, in the eighth century A.D., the woman mystic Rābi'a of Basra gave love a fundamental place in her thoughts. Her biographer 'Attār spoke of Rābi 'a as a woman on fire with love and ardent desire and consumed with her passion for God. She herself said, 'The groaning and the yearning of the lover of God will not be satisfied until it is satisfied in the Beloved.'[19] Rābi'a was one of the first Sufis to teach the disinterested love of God, without hope of reward or fear of punishment; she used to pray, 'O my Lord, if I worship thee from fear of Hell, then burn me in Hell, and if I worship thee from hope of Paradise, exclude me thence, but if I worship thee for thine own sake then withhold not from me thine eternal Beauty.'[20] This theme of love was continued by many Sufis, and was a prominent feature with the great Hallāj, as will be seen.

The other means of overcoming any separation of God from man lies in the very doctrine of the divine transcendence and omnipotence. It appears in the problems of predestination and freewill, where the basic belief was that since God alone is creator he creates all apparently human actions. Theologians eventually worked out a theory of 'acquisition' or appropriation, by which man appropriated what God had already done, so as to give man some moral responsibility for actions, but this only pushed the problem a stage further back, and in reality God was all and in all.

Similarly the doctrine of the unity of God was taken to mean not only that God was one Being, but that he was the only Being, the one true existent. If there did appear to be a gulf between God and man this was only in appearance, since again God was all and in all. A great student of Sufism, R. A. Nicholson, puts it thus:

> The infinite distance between God and man God alone can annihilate; man has no power to bridge the chasm, therefore it is overleaped by a *tour de force* of the omnipotent Will. That idea lies behind the whole theory and practice of religious ecstasy on

[19] M. Smith, *Rābi'a the Mystic*, 1928, p. 98.   [20] Ibid., p. 30.

which the Sūfīs throw so much stress. How should the mystic's conscious self not be obliterated and swept away by the transcendent glory of Him who in a sudden gleam reveals Himself as ineffably near?[21]

That such a theory of the sole divine unity and being could lead to monism, the identity of divine and human, appeared in the third Islamic century in Persia in the teachings attributed to Abū Yazīd, also called Bāyazīd or Bistāmī. He left no written work, but sayings are credited to him, such as, 'I became a bird with a body of unity', 'I saw the tree of unity'. Later biographers said that Abū Yazīd appeared before the throne of God and asked him, 'Adorn me with your unity'; this was so that when creatures saw him they would declare, 'We have seen you (namely, God), and you are *that*.' And seeking unity by casting off all personality Abū Yazīd cried out, 'Glory to me, how great is my majesty!'

Writers like Nicholson and Zaehner claim that Abū Yazīd was influenced by Indian pantheism. His teacher was a certain al-Sindi, which would seem to be Sind in India. 'You are That' is the famous phrase from the Chandogya Upanishad, though in Arabic 'that' is never used of God. Abū Yazīd spoke of a cosmic tree which resembles such a tree in the Upanishads and Bhagavad Gītā.[22]

It is true that many influences came into the Islamic world from India over the centuries. In mathematics the so-called 'Arabic' numerals were originally Indian; astronomy, astrology, trigonometry, romantic literature, ethics and philosophy all received inspiration from India. But this was mostly later, and in India itself, influencing the Mughal empire. In the early centuries influence was 'superficial', in such contacts India surprised Muslims but they did not try to understand it, and then contact ceased until the later imperial era. As for Buddhism, which was more missionary than Hinduism, there may have been some effect on the practical level but its theological, or Buddhological, ideas were too distant from Islam to be important.[23]

[21] R. A. Nicholson, *The Idea of Personality in Sūfism*, 1923, p. 13.
[22] R. C. Zaehner, *Hindu and Muslim Mysticism*, 1960, pp. 93 f.
[23] Massignon, op. cit., pp. 81 f.

MYSTICISM IN THE WORLD'S RELIGIONS

Whatever the truth of these arguments, Abū Yazīd and other Sufis must be studied within the Islamic context. It will have been noted that one central theme of his was 'unity'. The word used was *tawhīd*, which became a central technical term for Sufis, and is taken by some to be the very essence of Sufism as union with God. *Tawhīd* is an Arabic word meaning 'to make one' or 'to assert oneness'. It is applied in different ways to the oneness of God and theology is said to be the science of oneness which teaches that God has no partner or associates. But theologians went on to speak of God being oneness in himself, the only being that has absolute existence, and as we have seen it was not far from there to a more monistic assertion that God is all. Sufi practice of contemplation and ecstasy would reinforce the conviction of a unity in which distinctions of subject and object disappeared, and so monism could grow naturally within Islam. For some mystics indeed unity meant the isolation or separation of God from the created universe, thereby recreating a kind of dualism.

This was the theme of Junayd of Baghdad (d. 910), who opposed Abū Yazīd, but in championing Sufism as orthodox seems to have slipped into further difficulty. Junayd defined 'unity' as 'to separate the Eternal Essence from the originated essence', but he regarded the soul as the divine idea and as such eternal. It is dipped for a moment into the temporal world but it returns to the divine unity enriched by its experiences.[24]

A further important technical term was that of *fanā*, meaning 'oblivion' or 'annihilation', and applied to the obliteration of the soul in God. A Buddhist origin of this notion has been suggested in the annihilation of *nirvāna*, but *fanā* is into God and so others have suggested a Christian origin for it, though it seems to develop from Islamic principles. Junayd recognized three stages of *fanā*, as obliteration of characteristics, obliteration of pleasures, and obliteration of consciousness in attaining the vision of God in the final stage of ecstasy. But the self is not annihilated, as in Buddhism; it continues in God since even in the highest state the worshipper cannot apprehend the fullness of the deity. Junayd claimed that his

[24] A. H. Abdel-Kader, *The Life, Personality and Writings of al-Junayd*, 1962, pp. 68 f.

134

doctrine was neither incarnation in the Christian sense, nor deification, but it is a loss of will to find the eternal self in God. It must be said that not all Sufis made these fine distinctions.[25]

The most famous pupil of Junayd was the Persian mystic Hallāj, though the master thought his disciple spoke folly and nonsense in claiming to be intoxicated by God. Hallāj seems to have taken the doctrine of unity to extremes by declaring 'I am the Real' or 'the creative Truth', which was regarded as blasphemy since these were attributes of God alone. Hallāj was tortured and executed in Baghdad in 922, and he has been one of the most discussed Sufis ever since. He seems to have taught perfect union with God, through desire of and submission to suffering, and his biographers claimed that he followed the example of Jesus and prayed for his executioners. Jesus as a model of poverty and purity was often praised by Sufis, who regarded him as 'seal of the saints'.

Like many other Sufis Hallāj stressed the love of God, and it was this love which led him to unity expressed in one of his most famous verses:

I have become he whom I love, and he has become myself,
We are two spirits in one body,
When you see me you see him.

There is still a distinction of divine and human here but attempts are made to get beyond duality, into a union of will and spirit: 'His spirit is my spirit, what he wishes, I wish.' And more than this, for when man calls to God, it is God calling: 'When I saw the Lord with the eye of the heart and asked, Where are you? He replied, Yourself.'[26] Hallāj spoke of the divine and human spirits 'infused' into one body, and this word caused trouble because it was related to the term for 'incarnation', though most later Sufis denied that Hallāj used the term in any Christian sense.

Another great Persian mystic was Rūmī, and this country with its long traditions of different religions became one of the great centres of Sufi teaching and practice. Not only is Rūmī credited with the formation of the whirling dervishes, but his Mathnawi, 'couplets', a

[25] Ibid., pp. 81 f.
[26] L. Massignon, *Le Dīwān d'al-Hallāj*, 1955, pp. 41, 93.

vast poem in six books, has been called 'the Qur'ān in the Persian tongue', and many of its verses are known by heart by countless Persians to this day. Rūmī's version of unity is that in every age there is a manifestation of God, as Adam, Noah, Jesus and Muhammad. It was even 'he in human shape' that cried in Hallāj, 'I am the Real'. Jesus taught unity, a unicolority which was changed into diverse colours by his followers. The Shī'a Muslims taught that in every age there is an Imām, a spiritual leader, but this is the divine Guide, God himself. What may appear to be a succession of prophets and leaders, or a transmigration of souls, is in reality a series of manifestations of the divine unity.

Similarly the diversity of religions and sects hides the basic unity of religion, and in the love of God all are united:

> The lamps are different, but the Light is the same ... the disagreement between Moslem, Zoroastrian and Jew depends on the standpoint ...
> The two-and-seventy sects will remain till the Resurrection ...
> Love alone can end their quarrel, Love alone comes to the rescue when you cry for help against their arguments.[27]

Teaching the love of God, for all and in all, comes up against the problem of evil, and solves it in a way that appears right to some and too facile to others. Traditional Islam, following Christianity, taught a clear distinction of heaven and hell, but how could hell be everlasting if God was love? This problem has exercised modern theologians, but the mystics faced it long ago. Clearly nobody could be beyond the love of God forever, and perhaps those who seemed the most wicked were so in appearance only. Pharaoh hardened his heart against God and seemed to be lost, but Rūmī declared that 'both Moses and Pharaoh were worshippers of the Truth'. Moses worshipped God openly, while Pharaoh did so secretly and at night: 'Am I not praying all night long?' The most obdurate sinner might seem to be the devil, Iblīs, who according to the Qur'ān had been cast out of Paradise because he refused the divine command to bow down to Adam. But Rūmī taught that Iblīs refused to bow to Adam 'from love of God, not from disobedience', and so in fact he was the

[27] R. A. Nicholson, *Rūmī*, 1950, pp. 166, 173.

most faithful worshipper of God. Hence all creatures will be saved and united with the deity.[28]

There were many other Persian mystics, 'Attār, Hāfiz, Sa'dī and the like. To English readers Omar Khayyám is the best known, though through Fitzgerald's version this mathematician appears to have been more of a cynic or drunkard than a mystic. Yet in Persia Omar has long been regarded as a mystic, though not in the front rank. Sufis disregarded many conventions, and also often concealed their teachings under worldly or romantic verses, and wine, forbidden to the orthodox, was a common symbol of spiritual love. The best-known of Omar–Fitzgerald's verses runs:

> Here with a Loaf of Bread beneath the Bough,
> A Flask of Wine, a Book of Verse—and Thou
> Beside me singing in the Wilderness—
> And Wilderness is Paradise enow.[29]

It looks like an erotic picnic, but bread and wine have long been religious symbols, the Sufis composed many verses, retired to the desert, and sought union with 'thou' which was the best Paradise. Fitzgerald distorted some verses, and invented others, but Omar can be read in a mystical manner.

More famous than Omar as a Persian philosopher and mystic was Ghazālī in the eleventh century, hailed by some as 'the greatest Muslim since Muhammad', though by others with more reserve. He early became a professor of canon law at Baghdad but he tells us in his autobiography that traditional theology did not satisfy him but rather made him sceptical. Then he studied Sufi writings and abandoned his chair to travel to holy places and retreat centres, returning finally to teach and then to retire but in charge of a school and a Sufi monastery. Ghazālī said:

> I learnt that it is above all the mystics who walk on the road to God; their life is the best life, their method the soundest method, their character the purest character. . . . In general, then, how is a mystic 'way' (tarīqah) described? The purity which is the first

[28] R. A. Nicholson, Rūmī. pp. 145, 163.

[29] The Rubáiyát of Omar Khayyám, 11; see A. J. Arberry, The Romance of the Rubáiyát, 1959.

condition of it . . . is the purification of the heart completely from what is other than God most high; the key to it, which corresponds to the opening act of adoration in prayer, is the sinking of the heart completely in the recollection of God; and the end of it is complete absorption (*fanā'*) in God.[30]

Ghazālī emphasized unity (*tawhīd*) in the general sense of the unity of God, though in a Persian commentary attributed to him he argues that two things can never become one, so that if there appear to be two in reality there is only one, and 'perfect *tawhīd* means that nothing exists except the One'. In his exposition of this work Zaehner remarks that 'here at last Ghazālī forgets to worry about the orthodoxy he usually chooses to parade, and declares himself a non-dualist of whom Śankara might have been proud'.[31] However, despite some such passages in his later works the general view has been that Ghazālī made Sufism orthodox, or at least reconciled the orthodox teachers to its more moderate expressions.

At the other end of the Islamic world, born at Murcia in Spain in 1165, lived the most celebrated pantheistic mystic Ibn 'Arabī. He taught that there is nothing but God, who is manifested in countless forms. God is 'the One without oneness and the Single without singleness', he sees and knows himself by himself, there is no other than he and no existence than his.

Ibn 'Arabī quoted the words of the Gospel (though curiously he ascribed them to Moses) which said, 'I was sick and you did not visit me'. But he gave this a very different interpretation from the Gospel's, taking it to mean that the existence of the sick is God's existence, as all created things are his existence. Inevitably this leads to deification of humanity, or full monism.

When the mystery—of realizing that the mystic is one with the Divine—is revealed to you, you will understand that you are no other than God. . . . You will see all your actions to be his actions and all your attributes to be his attributes and your essence to be his essence.[32]

[30] W. M. Watt, *The Faith and Practice of al-Ghazālī*, 1953, pp. 60 f.
[31] R. C. Zaehner, *Hindu and Muslim Mysticism*, p. 166.
[32] R. Landau, *The Philosophy of Ibn 'Arabī*, 1959, pp. 83 f.

Yet despite this monistic identification Ibn 'Arabī, like many other Sufis, wrote love poetry to express the embodiment of divine love in a human ideal. A beautiful girl, called Nizām, was famed for her asceticism and eloquent preaching, and provided the Beatrice for this Dante. He wrote:

When she kills with her glances, her speech restores to life, as though she, in giving life thereby, were Jesus.

The smooth surface of her legs is like the Tora in its brightness, and I follow it and tread in its footsteps as though I were Moses.[33]

Despite the recognized conventions some of the orthodox were shocked at this eroticism, and Ibn 'Arabī was constrained to add lengthy commentaries to the poems, which are much less interesting though they do shed light on the complex symbolism that he uses.

Ibn 'Arabī's pantheism was attacked for heresy, but he had many followers and he is one of the most extreme representatives of that strain within Sufism which took the doctrine of unity to a conclusion that was certainly not the original sense. By the emphasis on the sole divine being, the nature of God becomes incomprehensible, without any real revelation, for even the divine emanations in saints and prophets are not really men. Whatever we may think of Ibn 'Arabī's doctrine of God, his doctrine of man is negligible, and perhaps the two go together.[34]

There have been many Sufis and Sufi orders down the ages, from wandering dervishes to highly organized communities, some of the latter holding strictly to poverty and independence of worldly authority, and others being luxurious and favoured by state rulers. Orders were often organized like trade guilds though they were religious communities led by holy men, and their spiritual fervour expressed itself in social work such as offering hospitality to travellers in monasteries, and caring for the poor and sick.

Down to the beginning of this century Sufi orders exercised a strong hold over the Islamic world, and there had been notable revivals in the nineteenth century, especially in Africa. But in modern times there have been open attacks on Sufi movements as well as more insidious undermining of their place in the contemporary

[33] Ibid., p. 92.   [34] See my *Avatar and Incarnation*, 1970, pp. 202 f.

world. The uneasy alliance between Sufism and orthodox theology was broken, and in attempts at purifying Islam by returning to its primitive purity Sufi practices were condemned as innovations. It must be said that popular Sufism was often full of superstition, and ragged dervishes, ecstatic dances and charlatan sheikhs have been attacked by reformers of Islam. In Turkey the orders were suppressed, though some survive under other names, and leaders in other Islamic countries have criticized Sufism for the superstition and stagnation of life in Islamic lands.

Sufi mystical principles and spiritual discipline have been less often attacked, though they have had few intellectual defenders. Muhammad Iqbal of the Punjab attempted a reconstruction of religious thought in Islam, which now seems exceedingly mild, and he wrote poems in a mystical spirit with the old Persian themes of roses and breezes, nightingales and houris, but there is little new or original. Yet at the popular level there is a vast amount of devotional literature which still comes from Sufi sources, and Constance Padwick has written finely of the religious themes in her collection of humble prayer books found half-buried under goods in grocers' shops.[35]

The Sufi orders have declined as much through urbanization and secularization as through direct attack, and where the sheikhs clung to the past they have been regarded as irrelevant for modern political and social movements. But the number of fully committed Sufis has always been a minority in Islam, and the mystical appeal will probably remain under modern conditions since, as we shall argue, there is a direct connection between the worship of the average believer and the mystical flights of the specialist. Trimingham, in his perceptive last chapter on the contemporary world, concludes: 'The Path, in our age as in past ages, is for the few who are prepared to pay the price, but the vision of the few who, following the way of personal encounter and commitment, escape from Time to know re-creation, remains vital for the spiritual welfare of mankind.'[36]

[35] C. Padwick, *Muslim Devotions*, 1961.
[36] J. S. Trimingham, *The Sufi Orders in Islam*, 1971, p. 259.

Chapter 12

CHRISTIAN DIVERSITY

NEW TESTAMENT MYSTICISM

It might have seemed natural to consider Christian mysticism after Judaism and come to Islam later, as presenting not only the historical order but also the spiritual continuity. It has been common in Christian theology and apologetic to present Christianity as a Semitic religion and a fulfilment of the Old Testament, yet a different viewpoint may be presented stressing both the universality and the radical new start of the *New* Testament. Hence J. S. Trimingham suggests that 'Islam, rather than Christianity, is the direct heir of all that is truest in Judaism, whose prophetic insights it has carried to greater heights, whilst at the same time discarding its limiting and exclusive elements. Islam may be regarded as the fulfilment of Judaism'.[1]

It is in its doctrines of God that Christianity differs from both Judaism and Islam, and we have seen that doctrines of God are vital for mysticism. It has been shown that neither Judaism nor Islam is entirely transcendental, but the emphasis on the 'Wholly Other' is present in them both, and monotheism in Christianity may be claimed as more dynamic and more immanental than in Judaism and Islam. Although theologians speak of the divine action 'from above' or Christ entering the world 'from without', this is too stark and transcendentalist a notion. The Christian doctrine of the Trinity, difficult though it may be, arose not out of speculation or theological systematization, but from experience of a fully immanental

---

[1] J. S. Trimingham, *Two Worlds are Ours*, 1971, p. 31.

relationship, as when Paul spoke of 'Christ in us, the hope of glory' which was the 'mystery among the Gentiles' (Col. 1.27).

In some ways Christian thought is closer to Indian than to Semitic monotheism. The Hindu avatar belief is the nearest that any religion shows to the Christian doctrine of the Incarnation, though each has its own distinctive features. The personal God of devotional Hinduism, and even the personal Buddha or Bodhisattva, are comparable with the personal Christ who formed the faith from the Resurrection onwards and has remained central to Christian mysticism down the ages. Of course Sufism within Islam has some affinity with the Indian world in theosophy but less than Christianity in its devotional links.

Yet while Christian mysticism has taught and sought ardently union with God it has nearly always avoided, again because of its trinitarian doctrine, that claim to identity of divine and human which was ever-present in Hinduism and a constant danger in Sufism. The Gospels teach the immanental presence of God, but personalized in Christ. 'The kingdom of God is within you' (Luke 17.21) or 'in your midst' and by his healings Christ shows 'the kingdom of God come upon you' (Luke 11.20). Christ is present 'where two or three are gathered together in my name' (Matt. 18.20) and at the end affirms 'I am with you always' (Matt. 28.20).

A closer relationship appears in the fourth Gospel with the long exposition on 'abide in me and I in you' (John 15.4), and this theme is developed by Paul, who claims, 'To me to live is Christ' and 'I live, and yet no longer I, but Christ lives in me' (Phil. 1.21; Gal. 2.20). Paul utters a wonderful Trinitarian mixture with 'Christ in you', 'The Spirit dwelling in you', 'The Spirit of God dwells in you', and 'The Spirit of Christ' (Rom. 8.2–11). This is both immanental and mystical in the highest degree, yet there is no identification in the sense of 'You are God'.

Christ is both the partner of mystical union and the prototype of union with the Father. Already in the Synoptic Gospels there is the statement, 'No one knows the Father except the Son' (Matt. 11.27). This has been called 'A bolt from the Johannine blue', and certainly it is taken further in the fourth Gospel in statements such as 'I and the Father are one' (John 10.30). Martin Buber has an interesting comment on this verse in which he contrasts it with Indian ideas of identification or absorption. John's Gospel, he says:

> is really the Gospel of pure relation. Here is a truer verse than the familiar mystical verse: 'I am Thou and Thou art I'. The Father and the Son, like in being—we may even say God and Man, like in being—are the indissolubly real pair, the two bearers of the primal relation, which from God to man is termed mission and command, and from man to God looking and hearing, and between both is termed knowledge and love.[2]

The Gospel, however, goes beyond this and sees the primal relation in the divine being itself, before that of God and man. The mystical union of the discourses at the Last Supper culminates in the prayer in John 17, 'that they may all be one, as thou Father art in me, and I in thee, that they also may be in us . . . that they may be one, as we are one, I in them and thou in me'. This is not merely an exhortation to Christian brotherhood, in some monolithic organization as plotted by ecclesiastical managers. It is a communion *within* the divine being which is not abstract or negative, and it is a communion *with* the divine being which is the closest unity without identity, because relationship requires distinction. The creed expressed later 'without distinction of persons' of God but not of man.

The New Testament provided the material, in text and experience, for constant debates in the early centuries over the nature of Christ. This resulted in the orthodox doctrines of divine and human natures in Christ, and the Trinity of Father, Son and Holy Spirit. These were not easy solutions but they helped to define the needs and the limits of Christian thought and devotion. If Christ was only a man he could not be that satisfying object of devotion that all Christian ages have demanded, and if he was not truly human the Incarnation was unreal. Unitarianism has had small appeal because it removed this devotion, and a Calvinist concentration upon the transcendence of God has appeared to deny his immanence personally in Christ and generally in the Spirit. Moreover the Incarnation gave the hope of the redemption of

[2] Martin Buber, *I and Thou*, p. 85.

fallen humanity through assumption into the divine nature, still without confusion of persons.

The second epistle of Peter promises that we may 'become partners of the divine nature' or 'share in the very being of God' (2 Pet. 1.4; New English Bible), and this is contrasted with the corruption of the world. Paul also spoke of God finally becoming 'all in all' (1 Cor. 15.28), and this is linked with the subordination of the Son to the Father but it is quite different from pantheistic monism. Christian theologians came to speak of Christ becoming human so that man might become divine, and Dionysius the Areopagite and other Eastern Orthodox wrote of the 'divinization' of human nature, but in the context of the doctrine of the Trinity.

Redeemed human nature is assumed into the Godhead, but is not its totality. Such a theme has remained in hymnology and congregations still sing Charles Wesley's words.

> Hear us, who thy nature share,
> Who thy mystic body are.

This is addressed to Christ, 'from whom all blessings flow', and it indicates the union of the worshipper with the Lord whose nature he shares as a member of the Church his body.

The doctrine of the Incarnation helped to check that flight into world-denial which has been a pervasive tendency in the mystical way. The early Upanishads affirm 'I am food', but later they speak of the world as full of disease and misery and praise renunciation of the desire for sons. The Buddha set out to solve the problem of suffering, and did so by rising aloof from secular life with a monkish order seeking Nirvāna. The Incarnation means the marriage of Spirit and Matter, in which 'the Word became flesh' and truly died on the Cross. Paul saw this need for the material world, despite some aversion, crying out, 'Who will deliver me from this body of death', but then affirming that 'the creation groans and travails in pain . . . awaiting the redemption of our body' (Rom. 7–8). It is not only the soul that is saved, with pie in the sky, but the body and the world, so that even after death there is a 'spiritual body'.

The New Testament uses marriage symbolism of union, and some writers have applied this to the union of the Virgin Mary with the Spirit of God in the divine conception, though the Bible does not develop this idea. Reference has been made (page 114) to the divine marriage of the Lamb and the Church, in the book of Revelation (Rev. 21.2 f.), but perhaps more significant and lasting in mystical influence is the teaching of the union of Christ with the church compared with that closest of unions, between husband and wife. 'Husbands love your wives, as Christ loved the Church and gave himself for it' (Eph. 5.25 f.). Later writers spoke of Christ as the divine Spouse and the soul as his Bride, and Protestant congregations have sung of 'Jesus, my Shepherd, Husband, Friend'.

It was noted at the beginning of this book that the word 'mystery' was used in the New Testament, especially by Paul who would know of its use in Greek mysteries. But all three Synoptic Gospels speak of 'the mystery of the kingdom of heaven' (Mark 4.11, etc.) and insist that the apparently simple parables have far deeper meanings which are revealed only to the few who find the hidden treasure and cherish the pearl of great price.

There is a gospel behind the gospels, or within and beyond them, and modern scholars do not usually follow the habit of an earlier generation and separate the 'Jesus of history' from the 'Christ of faith', since for all the New Testament writers Jesus was the Christ of faith, whose words they tried to record but whose presence they believed to be directly with them. The Johannine developments of the Feeding of the Five Thousand into teaching of the 'bread from heaven' must be understood in this light, for in Christian experience Jesus said, 'I am the bread of life, he that comes to me shall not hunger, and he that believes on me shall never thirst' (John 6.35). Even the apparently hard word, 'He that eats my flesh and drinks my blood has eternal life' (John 6.54), was immediately comprehensible to the Christian community that shared the bread-flesh and wine-blood of the Eucharist. It would be folly to interpret this as simple cannibalism, in which the disciples ate Jesus, as they never did, but there can be few closer mystical unions than taking food and drink into oneself. The Christian 'Holy Communion' is the supreme union in which 'He that eats my flesh and drinks my blood abides in me, and I in him'. These words are 'spirit and life'.

Finally, New Testament mysticism is conditioned throughout by the fundamental belief in the love of God, which is both transcendent and immanent. This is demonstrated in the words and acts of Jesus in the Synoptic Gospels, and worked out in theory in the Johannine and Pauline writings. 'God so loved the world' that he sent his Son, 'while we were yet sinners'. It is the divine initiative, which seeks out man for that union which is to 'abide in me, and I in you'. Because of this love of God, Christian mystical union looks outwards to others and produces loving actions. 'We love, because he first loved us', and 'If we love one another, God abides in us' (1 John 4.7 ff.).

The New Testament basis of Christian mysticism disproves the misguided attacks upon mysticism as self-salvation or an arrogant attempt of humanity to elevate itself into divinity. Such notions seem to lie behind Karl Barth's attacks on mysticism as 'esoteric atheism', when he discusses mysticism and atheism together in a section entitled 'Religion as Unbelief'.[3] Yet the initiative for mystical union comes from God, though man co-operates in the manner of the 'monkey-hold' of Vaishnavism (see p. 103) in a response of faith and love. With its roots in the New Testament, and never better expressed than in the Fourth Gospel, Christian mysticism grew and spread down the ages.

DEVELOPING MYSTICISM

The meeting of religions today is often regarded with alarm as likely to lead to 'syncretism', a mingling of religions which would contaminate an original purity. But Christianity is one of the most obvious and generally successful syncretisms, between Hebrew and Greek, and it is too late to cry in the manner of Zechariah, 'Thy sons, O Zion, against thy sons, O Greece' (Zech. 9.13). The complexity and diversity of the Christian tradition come from different strains, which were the price of its universal aims and began in the New Testament itself, written all in Greek and composed in different parts of the Mediterranean world. It was suggested earlier that Christian writers like Clement and Origen used terminology from the Greek mysteries for Christian teachers and ceremonies, and both the persecutions

[3] Karl Barth, *Church Dogmatics*. E.T., 1936, I, ii, 318 f.

CHRISTIAN DIVERSITY

which forced Christians into secret meetings, and the inner mystical teachings, enabled Christianity to enter into the heritage of the mysteries and expand them far and wide.

It has been common to discuss Eastern Orthodox theology and mysticism separately from Western Catholic, but the Orthodox Church regards itself as catholic and universal, and the formal division of East and West did not come till the eleventh century when it was as much attacks from the Western Crusades as doctrinal differences that caused the split. Eastern Christians owed much to the Western Augustine or Gregory the Great, as Westerns were indebted to Eastern teachers like Athanasius and Basil.

In Greek mystical theology, however, the term 'divinization' (*theosis*) is often used; we have met it already in the Syrian pseudo-Dionysius (p. 10) and some consideration must be given to it. Clearly this is not 'deification' (*apotheosis*) in the sense of the Roman custom of regarding emperors as gods, which Christians unanimously rejected. John of Damascus spoke of the interaction of nature and grace in restoring the perfection of man and uniting him progressively with the fullness of God, a 'divinization' which was the way to union with God. Gregory Nazianzen (329–389) spoke of God breathing in 'the divine part' of the soul so that it might receive the energy of God. Maximus the Confessor (580–662) showed how grace united human nature to become 'divine by grace', in contrast to Christ, who was divine by nature. Yet Christ is an example to us, and theological arguments against the division of the two natures in Christ were intended also to deny the division of man and God and affirm the ultimate union of human nature with divinity. The constant statement, 'What is not assumed, cannot be deified', had in mind both the deification of the human nature of Christ and the divinization of the whole human person. Human divinization, however, though a process begun here, cannot be consummated until the world to come, when God shall be all in all.[4]

The mystical way in the East was distinguished by different writers. For the pseudo-Dionysius there were two ways, of affirmation and unknowing, and three ways of spiritual life:

[4] V. Lossky, *The Mystical Theology of the Eastern Church*, 1957, pp. 126, 154, 196.

147

purgation, illumination and union. Isaac the Syrian, an ascetic writer of the seventh century, distinguished three stages on the way to union: penitence that is conversion of the will, purification that liberates from the passions, and perfection that is perfect love through grace. In Hesychasm, 'quietism', the mystical system taught by the monks of Mount Athos from the fourteenth century, emphasis was placed upon ascetic practices, quiet of body and mind, and attainment of the vision of the Uncreated Light of God. Breathing exercises were used which had some resemblance to Yoga, and concentration was fixed by repetition of the Jesus-prayer: 'Lord Jesus Christ, Son of God, have mercy on me'. There was considerable controversy over disciplines and doctrines, particularly over a distinction made between God's essence and his light, but for centuries Hesychasm was virtually identified with Orthodoxy.[5]

In the West there were also many mystical teachers and movements, monastic movements, which sought to ensure perfection more easily than in the world, began in the East in the third-fourth century with Antony of Egypt and his successors. Monastic orders generally followed the Counsels of Perfection in the vows of poverty, chastity and obedience, which could be followed in the world but more fully in organized communities. In the West it was Benedict, 'the Patriarch of western monasticism', who in the sixth century formulated his rule, originally intended for lay monks, which became for centuries the dominant rule of monastic life, of work, study and prayer.

In the development of mystical doctrine there is special interest for this study in the teachings of Meister Eckhart, the thirteenth-century German Dominican, because he is quoted endlessly as one clear example of the monistic or pantheistic within Christian mysticism. Eckhart was one of the leaders of a great period in German mysticism, which included well-known mystics like Suso, Tauler and Thomas à Kempis. Suso said that in the 'highest stage of union' all consciousness of self disappears and 'the soul is plunged into the abyss of the Godhead, and the soul has become one with God'.

Eckhart was accused of going further, and although he defended himself during his life, many of his statements were condemned after his death. Most of his works are lost, but better acquaintance with

[5] Ibid., pp. 208 f.

what remains has led to modern reaction in his favour. Eckhart said that if a man does well 'God is really in him, and with him everywhere, on the streets and among people, just as much as in church, or a desert place, or a cell. If he really has God, and only God, then nothing disturbs him. . . . The whole business of his person adds up to God.'⁶ This is immanence but not pantheism. Or again, 'God enters the soul with all he has and not in part. He enters the soul through its core and nothing may touch that core except God himself'.

In his *Defence* Eckhart discussed the interpretation of biblical verses which had been attributed to him. On Romans 8, being 'conformed to the image of his Son', he remarks, 'It does not follow that we are God, as in Christ the first-born man is God, begotten the idea and likeness of the Father-God—for we are born *after* the idea and likeness and created'. And again, 'No man, however holy and good, becomes Christ himself, or First Begotten, nor are others saved through him, nor is he the likeness of God, the only begotten Son of God: but he is *after* the likeness of God, a part of him who is truly and perfectly the Son.'⁷ Despite vague allusions and ambiguities it seems that trinitarian doctrine saved Eckhart from an undifferentiated monism.

There were comparable expressions among mystics in fourteenth-century England. Contrary to the notion that the English are an unimaginative and unmystical people, one may refer to the wealth of lyrical poetry and to many mystics, so numerous that when Rudolf Otto lectured in this country he remarked that to speak of mysticism here was like carrying coals to Newcastle. When the *Mystical Theology* of Dionysius was translated into English it is said that it 'ran across England like a deer'. A famous anonymous English mystical treatise of the fourteenth century, the *Cloud of Unknowing*, was perhaps composed by the translator of what he called *Diònise Hid Divinite*. The negative mysticism of Dionysius, which held the impossibility of knowing God by unaided reason, is specifically quoted in the *Cloud*, though only towards the end: 'Saint Denis said: the most goodly knowing of God is that, the which is known by unknowing.'

⁶ R. B. Blakney, tr., *Meister Eckhart*, 1941, pp. 7 f., 97.
⁷ Ibid., 297, 268.

The *Cloud* teaches that there is a darkness 'and as it were a cloud of unknowing' between man and God, so that he can neither be seen clearly by reason nor be felt by love. Nevertheless, the contemplative should 'beat evermore on this cloud of unknowing', with 'a sharp dart of longing love'. And later it is said that perhaps God will sometimes send out a beam of spiritual light, 'piercing this cloud of unknowing that is between thee and him, and show thee some of his secret'.[8]

The *Cloud* discusses how the soul can be 'oned' with God, a pleasant English term used by other writers of the time, though not much is said about it till near the end of this book. Man may attain by grace what he cannot have by nature, 'that is to say, to be oned to God, in spirit, and in love, and in accordance of will'. But this 'oneing' is unity yet not identity of man and God, for 'thou art beneath thy God'. He is God by nature, without beginning, and man was once nothing in substance, later fell into sin, and only by grace is he oned with God for ever. So that, 'although thou art all one with him in grace, yet thou art full far beneath him in nature'.[9]

Somewhat earlier than the *Cloud*, Richard Rolle of Yorkshire was one of the first religious authors to write in English as well as Latin and he has been called 'the true father of English literature'. Until the Reformation Richard Rolle was the most widely read of all the English mystics, though he was a layman, and his warmth and sincerity made him attractive. Richard Rolle wrote especially of the love of God, the love of the Trinity and the love of Christ. No man can love God too much, he said, and in his most famous work *The Fire of Love*, he speaks eight hundred times of loving God, in terms like these:

> Jesu, when I am in you, and on fire with joy,
> and when the heat of love is surging in,
> I want to embrace you, the most loving,
> with my whole being.[10]

This is mystical union and almost erotic, yet it is agapé, and if one is reminded of the female raptures of Teresa of Avila there are many

[8] *The Cloud of Unknowing*, ed. E. Underhill, 1946 edn, pp. 189, 50, 75, 105.
[9] Ibid., p. 183.
[10] Richard Rolle, *The Fire of Love*, modernized by C. Wolters, 1972, p. 154.

more parallels in male mystics like Bernard of Clairvaux on the Song of Songs. Richard Rolle was a celibate anchorite, but it will be seen later that the married Charles Wesley wrote as passionately of the divine love.

Walter Hilton, perhaps a little later than the *Cloud*, in his *Scale of Perfection* writes, but only occasionally, about this oneness. Significantly, first of all it embraces the church, 'for God and Holy Church are so oned and accorded together that whoso acts against one acts against both'. Then the unification is effected through Jesus, and the soul 'shall see mankind in the person of Jesus above the kind of angels oned to the Godhead'. Hilton regards Jesus as the light and union of the soul. 'He is in your soul and never shall be lost out of it. . . . He is in you, though he be lost from you; but you are not in him till you have found him.' Once again there is a difference between divine and human, though the goal is union. 'As long as Jesus finds not his image reformed in you, he is strange and far from you,' but his likeness results in charity, which is 'to love your fellow-Christian as yourself'. Therefore 'every reasonable soul ought with all its might to covet nighing to Jesus and oneing with him, through feeling his gracious and invisible presence'.[11]

More plainly than either the *Cloud* or Hilton, though perhaps influenced by them, and at the end of the same fourteenth century in England, the *Revelations of Divine Love* by the Lady Julian of Norwich emphasize the oneness of the soul and God. For Julian, God is everything to us, our clothing that wraps, clasps and encloses us in love. 'Till I am substantially oned to him, I may never have full rest or true bliss; that is to say, till I am so fastened to him that nothing that is made is between my God and me.' There is a distinction between divine and human, for even 'if the soul is ever like to God in kind and substance, restored by grace, it is often unlike in condition, by sin on man's part, and so it is prayer that ones the soul to God'. Then 'our soul is so fully oned to God of his own goodness that nothing at all may be between God and our soul'.[12]

[11] Walter Hilton, *The Scale of Perfection*, modernized edn, 1927, pp. 108, 94 f., 367.
[12] Mother Julian, *Revelations of Divine Love*, ed. G. Warrack, 1934, pp. 10, 90, 97.

151

Julian uses many examples. Christ and our Lady were 'so oned in love that the greatness of her loving was the cause of the greatness of her pain', and the 'great oneing between Christ and us' implies that when he was in pain we were in pain. Unusually for a Christian writer the Lady Julian writes of the female as well as the male side of the deity. God is our Father, but he is also our Mother, he is further 'our true Spouse and our soul is his loved Wife'. God made us all at once, and 'in our making he knit us and oned us to himself, by which oneing we are kept as clear and as noble as we were made'. God works continually to knit us to himself, so that 'in the knitting and the oneing he is our Very, True Spouse, and we his loved Wife, his Fair Maiden'. God is the Midpoint of everything. All that is made is like a hazel-nut in the palm of the hand. He dwells in the soul as in an honourable city, for the soul is as large as an endless world where Jesus, God and Man, has his endless dwelling.[13]

Time would fail to discuss even the major Western European mystics, English and Irish, German and Netherlands, Italian and French, but brief reference may be made to Spain, and especially to Teresa and John of the Cross for some words on that union with God which has been our special concern. Teresa's experiences are well known, and her visions will be referred to again later. She claimed to have reached a state of spiritual union with God and spiritual marriage, yet she was careful to limit her descriptions. There is a union which is spiritual betrothal and one which is marriage. 'Although union means that two things are joined together in one, yet in fact they may separate, and each may remain alone, as we frequently see, for the grace of union with our Lord passes quickly.' This union of betrothal is like two candles joined together, so that their light is one, yet they may be separated, one candle from the other or the wick from the wax. But spiritual marriage may be compared to rain falling into a river, where the waters are united and can no more be separated, or like a stream falling into the sea which can no longer be distinguished; a similar comparison to the monistic parable in the Chāndogya Upanishad (6.10). Yet Teresa is careful to say that the divine marriage 'cannot be consummated in perfection while we live here below', for we can still separate ourselves from

[13] Ibid., pp. 40, 122, 167.

God and lose that supreme blessing. In this life, however, 'it is impossible to say more than this: that so far as can be understood, the soul, I mean the spirit of this soul, becomes one thing with God'.[14]

John of the Cross, a younger contemporary of Teresa, in Spain of the sixteenth century, is noted for his doctrines of the 'ascent' and the 'dark night' of the soul. The soul is purified by the 'night of the senses' and becoming detached from outward forms it subsists in pure faith. Then there is a 'night of the spirit', a second purification, usually with intense suffering. Finally there is union, in 'the living flame of love'. John of the Cross is generally regarded as an austere saint, teaching utter abandonment of forms and helps in 'nothingness, nothingness, nothingness'. Yet his writings are classics of Spanish literature, and his poems in particular breathe both beauty and devotion. Here the unity of the soul with God is seen to follow the example of the divine unity in the Trinity, an important example for mystics of both East and West in Christianity.

> As Belovèd in the Lover
> one in the other resides,
> so the love that makes them one
> the same in each abides.
>
> With the one and with the other
> there was equality,
> So three Persons, one Belovèd,
> loved all and they were three.
>
> There was one love in all of them,
> and one the Lover gives
> both to Lover and Belovèd,
> in each of whom he lives.[15]

PROTESTANT MYSTICS

W. T. Stace is said to have declared once that 'there are no Protestant mystics'.[16] I have not been able to trace this statement and

[14] Teresa of Avila, *The Interior Castle*. E.T., anon., 1945, pp. 107 f.

[15] St John of the Cross, *Poesias*, IX.

[16] Quoted in A. Fremantle, *The Protestant Mystics*, 1965, p. xi.

it is strange, since in his *Mysticism and Philosophy* Stace quoted 'examples from Catholic and Protestant Christianity'. But when W. H. Auden and Anne Fremantle set out to prove that there were Protestant mystics, they discovered that many Protestants agreed with Stace's first statement. 'Calvinists, *en masse*, thought that even if there were mystics, there shouldn't be any; other Protestants claimed ... that only the Society of Friends could claim genuine Protestant mystics.'[17]

R. C. Zaehner had also written of 'the Protestant suspicion of mysticism', though he admitted that it should not amount to an outright rejection, since that would entail ignoring the prayer of Christ, 'that they may all be one in us'. Yet in the previous paragraph he had maintained that not only Judaism but 'the main stream of Protestantism' is 'anti-mystical', and for the same reason, 'each is exclusively obsessed by the transcendent holiness of God and man's nothingness in face of Him'.[18] It is not clear what is meant by the 'main stream' of Protestantism. Is it perhaps the Calvinism of Zaehner's forefathers, which may have driven him into Roman Catholicism? Certainly many lifelong Protestants would deny this 'exclusive obsession' and 'nothingness'.

Yet another writer, H. P. Owen, a Presbyterian, perhaps from a Calvinistic 'mainstream', has maintained that 'Christians of the "twice-born" type (especially evangelical Protestants) have often been strongly anti-mystical'.[19] In fact, it is the twice-born type of Protestants who have provided some of the most mystical writers, as study of their literature would show, and this is illustrated later. Much of the genius of Protestantism is expressed in its hymnology, which reveals the close association of art with mysticism. Not only in German Pietism, though notably there, but in much other evangelical Protestantism there are many expressions of the love of God, immanent as well as transcendent, and aspirations after communion and union with him.

In their anthology of *The Protestant Mystics* Auden and Fremantle assembled a very mixed company. Luther is there but no

[17] Ibid., loc. cit.
[18] R. C. Zaehner, *At Sundry Times*, p. 171.
[19] H. P. Owen, 'Christian Mysticism', in *Religious Studies*, 1971, pp. 40 f.

Calvin, though the Calvinist Jonathan Edwards appears. Boehme and Swedenborg are there, of course, but also Bunyan and Baxter. The Anglican poets Herbert, Vaughan and Traherne figure largely, and also the nature poets Blake, Wordsworth and even Keats. John Wesley is here, but not Charles, an omission that we shall remedy. Here are the Quakers George Fox and John Woolman, and the Americans Emerson, Thoreau, Whitman and Hudson. Even Van Gogh and Virginia Woolf are included, and of moderns there are T. S. Eliot, John Betjeman and Dietrich Bonhoeffer.

It is indeed a catholic collection, and it might be objected that anybody is liable to be called a mystic. But if the question is enlarged, to ask whether these writers can justly be regarded as religious or spiritual, then clearly a wide definition is essential. It has been argued, and will be again, that the distinction between spiritual and mystical experience is artificial, and is a matter of degree rather than of kind. Writers who teach communion with God, or union or identity, may all be regarded as seeking mystical union, though the differences between them are important.

Protestantism, we hold, is neither unmystical nor anti-mystical, but its mysticism may be expressed in different ways and by different classes of people than some of the Christian mystics we have been considering. Most mystics of East and West in medieval times who took a prominent part in teaching and counsel were monks or nuns. These were the specialists, who had time to develop their doctrines, though it was not denied that lay people could attain to spiritual union, and some like Catharine of Genoa (1447–1510) remained in the world and cared for the sick. After the Reformation, with abolition of the monasteries, most expert spiritual teaching was given by the clergy. But there were lay writers also, and mystical elements may be found in poetry as well as in manuals of spiritual counsel. Three centuries after the mystics of the fourteenth century, there was another burst of devotional writing in England, chiefly in verse, among the so-called 'metaphysical' poets. Some of the seventeenth-century poets were laymen and some were clergy. The earliest, John Donne, a Dean of St Paul's, has few original theological doctrines. He speaks of God as 'that All, which always is All everywhere', the 'cornerless and infinite', and for the best prayer he chooses darkness:

> To see God only I go out of sight,
>> And to 'scape endless days I choose
>> An everlasting night.

More interesting from a mystical point of view was Francis Quarles, a layman and popular in his lifetime but neglected afterwards, though he was championed by Charles Lamb. His *Emblems* have quaint passages, but there are verses on the union of God and man, like this:

> E'en so we met; and after long pursuit
>> E'en so we join'd, we both became entire;
> No need for either to renew a suit,
>> For I was flax, and he was flames of fire.
> Our firm united souls did more than twine;
> So I my best beloved's am; so he is mine.

'Holy George Herbert', a country parson, is better known, but he is more penitential and anguished than mystical. Yet he does write of the absence of God which excels all distance, and of his nearness 'making two one' (*The Search*), and of love triumphing over guilt in 'Love bade me welcome'.

Henry Vaughan, a doctor, is noted for his vision of eternity as a ring for the sacred marriage:

> I saw Eternity the other night
>> Like a great ring of pure and endless light . . .
> This ring the Bridegroom did for none provide
>> But for his Bride.

Another of Vaughan's poems recalls the divine Darkness of Dionysius or the *Cloud of Unknowing*. It is significantly entitled *Night*:

> There is in God—some say—
> A deep, but dazzling darkness . . .
> O for that Night! where I in him
> Might live invisible and dim.

But of all these seventeenth-century English Protestant poets it is in the work of Thomas Traherne, a clergyman, that appear some of the finest and most diverse expressions of mystical thought. His poems and prose writings remained in manuscript and almost lost for two hundred years and only in this century have been published. While perhaps Traherne's admirers were too enthusiastic yet by reaction he may have been later undervalued, especially for his original religious expressions. His poems are mystical, but world-affirming, and full of bursts of joy:

> The World resembled his Eternity
>   In which my Soul did walk;
> And everything that I did see
>   Did with me talk . . .
> . . . I within did flow
>   With Seas of Life like Wine;
> I nothing in the world did know
>   But 'twas divine.   (*Wonder*)

Traherne's prose writings are even more impressive, and the most frequently quoted passage from his *Centuries of Meditations* expresses the same joy in the world and unity with God:

Your enjoyment of the world is never right, till every morning you awake in Heaven: see yourself in your Father's Palace; and look upon the skies, the earth, and the air as Celestial Joys. . . .

You never enjoy the world aright, till the Sea itself floweth in your veins, till you are clothed with the heavens, and crowned with the stars: and perceive yourself to be the sole heir of the whole world, and more than so, because men are in it who are every one sole heirs as well as you.[20]

Traherne's perception of the unity of all beings, in and with God, continues throughout his work. 'How happy we are that we may live in all, as well as one; and how all-sufficient Love is, we may see by this: The more we live in all, the more we live in one.' Traherne asks: 'How can God be Love unto himself, without the imputation of self-love?' and he answers: 'His love unto himself is his love unto men, and his love unto them is love unto himself.' And again: 'God is to dwell in us, and we in him, because he lives in our knowledge and we

[20] T. Traherne, *Centuries of Meditations*, 1, 28–9.

in his. His will is to be in our will, and our will is to be in his will, so that both being joined and becoming one, we are pleased in all his works as he is.'[21]

In an earlier *Century* Traherne had prayed: 'O let me so long eye thee, till I be turned into thee, and look upon me till thou art formed in me, that I may be a mirror of thy brightness, a habitation of thy love, and a temple of thy glory. That all thy saints might live in me, and I in them; enjoying all their felicities, joys and treasures.'[22] Traherne has been suspected of pantheism, but Paul had spoken of Christ being 'formed in you' (Gal. 4.19) and this prayer of Traherne's is directed to Jesus, king of saints. Here, as in Christian mysticism generally, the personal imagery and the trinitarian assumptions prevent a monistic doctrine.

In eighteenth-century England there arose the Methodist movement, with little doctrinal innovation but reacting to the Industrial Revolution and seeking to cater for the religious needs of the unchurched masses. Methodism was accused of enthusiasm but not often of mysticism, yet since it became a powerful part of the 'main stream' of Protestantism it is worth mentioning its mystical tendencies.

John Wesley, an Anglican clergyman, and one of the chief founders of early Methodism, is often quoted as opposed to mysticism. The Oxford English Dictionary gives his statement that 'the same poison of Mysticism . . . has extinguished the last spark of life'. But that was written in reaction against the passivity of some Pietists, and perhaps also the speculations of Boehme. Yet Wesley was profoundly influenced by Moravian Pietism, from his 'twice born' conversion in 1738, and throughout his life, though as an active evangelist he deplored such quietism as renounced the very means of grace which should have nurtured piety. At least on a broad definition of mysticism, as communion or union with God, Wesley always showed himself mystical, and this comes out especially in his hymns, many of them translations from German Pietists like Tersteegen. The influence of these hymns, much more than Wesley's sermons or commentaries, was great on the whole

[21] Ibid., 2, 61; 4, 65; 4, 72.
[22] Ibid., 1, 87.

movement, and for two centuries lay Methodist men and women have sung such mystical words as these, translated by John Wesley:

> Thou hidden love of God, whose height,
>   Whose depth unfathomed, no man knows,
> I see from far thy beauteous light,
>   Inly I sigh for thy repose;
> My heart is pained, nor can it be
> At rest, till it find rest in thee.[23]

But it was his brother Charles Wesley, also a clergyman but 'twice born', who was the great singer of the movement and wrote over six thousand hymns. His hymns, which are often confused with his brother's few translations, show a great range of doctrine and piety, and they are essentially orthodox, stressing the great doctrines of the Church. It is one of the more pleasing features of modern ecumenism that two recent Roman Catholic hymnals have included some of Charles Wesley's hymns and that, apart from translations and modern writings, he is the author most often quoted.

Charles Wesley's hymns are very wide-ranging. On the personal, symbolical or visionary, side he is an ardent mystic. His devotion to the person of Christ has something of that feminine quality which Protestants have lacked through absence of devotions to the Virgin Mary. A popular hymn, full of imagery and passion, links ancient Israel with Christian mystical union:

> Thou Shepherd of Israel, and mine,
>   The joy and desire of my heart,
> For closer communion I pine,
>   I long to reside where thou art.

And it concludes, after describing the ecstasy of gazing on God:

> 'Tis there I would always abide
>   and never a moment depart,
> Concealed in the cleft of thy side,
>   eternally held in thy heart.[24]

There are innumerable other hymns with similar themes and Charles Wesley, as an advanced mystic, goes on from communion to

[23] *The Methodist Hymn Book*, 1933, 433.   [24] Ibid., 457.

159

union. This appears, significantly no doubt, in one of his masterpieces on the Incarnation. He begins by speaking of:

> Our God contracted to a span,
> incomprehensibly made man.

It is probably apocryphal, but it has been said that when Wesley had written those words, 'incomprehensibly made man', he laid down his pen and remarked, 'Beat that if you can'. He proceeded to show both the separation from God, caused by sin, and the reconciliation effected in Christ which made man a 'partaker of the divine nature'.

> He deigns in flesh to appear,
> widest extremes to join,
> To bring our vileness near
> and make us all divine;
> And we the life of God shall know,
> For God is manifest below.

The surprising last lines, which indicate unity if not absorption into God, are reinforced in the final verse:

> Then shall his love be fully showed,
> And man shall then be lost in God.[25]

But there is an even more extraordinary example in which Wesley seems to verge on monism, though probably not of the Śankara type. This appears in a hymn to the Holy Spirit, of which one verse ends:

> Plunged in the Godhead's deepest sea
> and lost in thine immensity.[26]

No doubt Charles Wesley, as a devotional but not a systematic theologian, would have justified his flights of poetical mysticism. But they are not without parallel, and in the nineteenth century the High Church John Keble wrote in 'Sun of my soul' lines which have been sung ever since,

> Till in the ocean of thy love
> we lose ourselves in heaven above.

[25] Ibid., 142.   [26] Ibid., 299.

Hymns are important, not simply for the reputation of the writer but for the effect they have on popular devotion. For two centuries Methodists, and many other Protestants, have sung the Wesleyan flights of mystical aspiration, and they have been translated into many languages, including African, so that they have given expression to the mysticism of the ordinary believer.

The extent of Christian mysticism is so vast that all we have been able to do is to indicate certain themes that are of interest because of comparisons elsewhere, try to correct some misapprehensions, and suggest some places where mysticism has flourished almost unnoticed.

A standard Christian dictionary defines mysticism as 'in general, an immediate knowledge of God attained in this present life through personal religious experience. It is primarily a state of prayer and as such admits of various degrees from short and rare Divine "touches" to the practically permanent union with God in the so-called "mystic marriage".' The author recognizes that mysticism is widespread in many religions, but suggests two distinctive forms of Christian mysticism. The first is in contrast to 'pan-cosmic' conceptions of Reality and holds that this Reality transcends the cosmos and the soul. The second is that in place of notions of the absorption of the soul into the divine, Christian mysticism teaches a union of love and will which always retains the distinction between the Creator and the creature.[27] This is true, generally speaking, though we have noticed that not all mystical writers are careful to maintain these distinctions. But, in the main, trinitarian conceptions of God have enabled Christian mystics to speak of union without identity, and emphasis upon loving relationships reinforces this. It has been observed that there is no love for isolated monads in Sāmkhya or Jain philosophy, whereas love assumes some duality both in *bhakti* and in Christian mysticism.

[27] 'Mysticism' in *The Oxford Dictionary of the Christian Church*, ed. F. L. Cross, 1958 edn.

PART IV

Experience

Chapter 13

VISIONS, RAPTURES AND SEX

VISIONS

Some modern authorities completely exclude certain unusual experiences from their descriptions of mysticism, while others more moderately regard such states as preliminary, dispensable, or far from constituting the whole of mystical life. Although popular opinion may regard visions and voices as mystical, and many well-known mystics have been subject to such experiences, yet that a man claims to hear voices, or to be able to raise himself from the ground by invisible means, or to have a third eye, does not prove that he is a mystic. He may be a charlatan or a liar.

Zaehner says roundly that the mystical experience 'has nothing to do with visions, auditions, locutions, telepathy, telekinesis, or any other praeternatural phenomenon which may be experienced by saint and sinner alike and which are usually connected with an hysterical temperament.'[1] Yet according to all the Gospels Jesus himself had visions and locutions, at the baptism, in the desert, at the transfiguration and at Jerusalem, and he would hardly be called hysterical. Paul claimed to have 'visions and revelations of the Lord'; he both saw and heard Christ when his companions had no such experience, and he claimed to be caught up to the third heaven to hear unspeakable words. Countless other mystics have had similar experiences, which they would not have described as 'subsidiary, accidental, parasitic',[2] but more likely as vocational, introductory and leading to more ineffable revelations.

[1] R. C. Zaehner, *Mysticism, Sacred and Profane*, p. 32.   [2] loc. cit.

That 'saint and sinner' can have such experiences may indicate that a hard and fast line should not be drawn between them, that all men and women have a capacity for the supernatural, and that some pursue the experience to a deeper conclusion while others do not. Zaehner affirms that people in a state of grace do not look different, or behave differently, from those who may be in mortal sin, though one might think that the behaviour ought to be different. But the mystic, he says, *knows* that God is with him and in him, and that is the experienced fact, that is the mystical state, that is distinctive. So be it, but the vision may minister to it, introduce it, confirm it, and be part of it.

W. T. Stace approached his definition of mysticism by exclusion, declaring that 'visions and voices are not mystical phenomena', apparently because they are sensuous, whereas the most important type of mystical experience is non-sensuous. He admits that popular opinion may regard visions and voices as mystical, but decides that they must not be confused with genuine mysticism, even when experienced by recognized great mystics.[3] He holds that Paul's experiences of light and a voice on the road to Damascus should not 'as such' be classed as mystical, though his vision of the third heaven later has a 'more mystical ring'. Stace agreed that Teresa often saw visions, but 'she was not an intellectual' like Eckhart, and it is wiser to follow the advice of John of the Cross and not seek to be 'encumbered' by visions if the soul wishes to 'remain detached, empty, pure and simple'. At the higher and later stages of experience visual and auditory events tend to be transcended in a more refined and indescribable communion with the divine. But it seems arbitrary to exclude popular experience, and to make a divide between the less intellectual and the more so, and between preliminary and advanced experience.

Stace quotes from versions of the Upanishads as 'invariably' describing 'mystical experiences' as 'soundless, formless, intangible', and he seems to be unaware that these adjectives are applied to the soul or self (*ātman*), discernment of which brings liberation.[4] In a further quotation many words are added: 'As you practise

[3] W. T. Stace, *Mysticism and Philosophy*, pp. 47 f.
[4] Katha Upanishad, 3.15; Śvetāśvatara, 2.11.

meditation you may see in visions forms . . . fire, smoke, wind,' etc. The Upanishad says that these are preliminary appearances, but Stace claims that they are distinct from the genuine mystical state, though it might be better to regard them as the first or introductory part of it.

Supernatural visions and voices are not experienced by all men and women, probably only by a minority, so that in a sense they could be called abnormal although they are commonly mentioned in religious literature, including the mystical. More universal are dreams, which modern psychology has taught us not to ignore, and which many scriptures have considered to be vehicles of divine communication with man. Indeed it is difficult to distinguish between visions and dreams in many cases.

The standard life of Muhammad says that when he was in a cave on Mount Hira the angel Gabriel came to him 'while I was asleep', but then he awoke and saw 'Gabriel in the form of a man with feet astride the horizon'.[5] Similarly the four dreams reported in the first two chapters of Matthew's Gospel could just as easily have been visions, for 'an angel appeared' or a warning came. Those who dismiss or ignore belief in God may regard all such experiences, visions or dreams, as superficial and the mere result of free association. But to the eye of faith, as to many psychologists, the dream brings revelation and perhaps warning. If a dream or vision is of an angel or a dead person it is not necessarily communion with God, but it may be preparatory to such deeper experience and should not be dismissed out of hand as having nothing to do with mysticism.

Visions may not come to most of us, or they may occur in times of stress or physical disturbance, and might then be dismissed as diseased. C. G. Jung related visions that came to him in a state of unconsciousness, after a heart attack and when he was being given injections. But far from dismissing these fantasies as diseased or trivial, the psychologist in his characteristic manner gave them close clinical attention in later reflection and analysis. In his autobiography Jung gave an outline of these experiences and concluded that 'it is impossible to deny the beauty and intensity of emotion during these visions. They were the most tremendous things

5 *The Life of Muhammad*, tr. A. Guillaume, p. 106.

I have ever experienced.' He insisted that these experiences were not delusions or caused by disease. 'It was not a product of the imagination; there was nothing subjective about them; they all had a quality of absolute objectivity. We shy away from the word "eternal", but I can describe the experience only as the ecstasy of a non-temporal state in which present, past, and future are one.'[6]

It might be objected that Jung was not a mystic, and he did not claim to be an orthodox Christian though he believed that Christianity was necessarily the religion for Europe. He has been criticized as more preoccupied with magic than religion, though it is difficult to separate the two, and Jung's interest in alchemy was aroused by its symbolism and parallels with his psychology of the unconscious. Yet Jung was one of the most outstanding lay writers on religion in this century, and the width and originality of his approach to religion are important. Jung spoke of the experience of God as the basic human experience, and he wrote of knowing God 'as a hidden, personal, and at the same time supra-personal secret'. He claimed to have a 'mystical participation' with other people, so that he could see them as they were without deception, and he considered that Freud's obsession with sex expressed a flight 'from that other side of him which might perhaps be called mystical'.[7]

Experiences of visions and voices and other phenomena have been counted as part of mystical life, not simply by the populace at large but among devout followers of most religions. It may help towards tidy definition to exclude everything that does not fit into categories of pantheistic or theistic, introvertive or extravertive mysticism, but mystical life is far more diverse. Certainly there are dangers and it is necessary, as the apostle said, to 'prove the spirits, whether they are of God'. But he did not deny the spirits and their role in religious life, and the New Testament is not afraid of diversity. Among the gifts of the Spirit are wisdom and faith, but also healings and miracles, tongues and locutions, and discernment of spirits. These are 'praeternatural phenomena', communications of the divine essence, and truly mystical.

Moderate opinion recognizes that psycho-physical phenomena

[6] C. G. Jung, *Memories, Dreams, Reflections.* E.T. Fontana edn, 1967, p. 326.
[7] Ibid., pp. 62, 68, 175.

have been 'frequent concomitants of mystical experience', and these are recognized by Christian spiritual writers as accessories to true mystical insight. On the other hand, such experiences are not essential to the mystical state, they may be hindrances to it, and in the highest states they may cease altogether.[8]

RAPTURES AND SEX

Stace also discounts 'raptures, trances, and hyper-emotionalism'. Teresa gave notable accounts of raptures, which either brought her great stillness, or occasioned extreme bodily pain. But she also spoke of passing beyond such states into the peace of union with God. Such raptures can easily be criticized, or explained away, if the subjects are celibate women who can be called sex-starved, but they are more difficult to account for in a well-married man like Muhammad, and some account was given earlier of his visions and trance states (pp. 121–8).

Teresa's famous vision is worth quoting to see precisely what she says, and does not say.

Our Lord was pleased that I should sometimes see a vision of this kind. Beside me, on the left hand, appeared an angel in bodily form, such as I am not in the habit of seeing except very rarely. Though I often have visions of angels, I do not see them. . . . In his hands I saw a great golden spear, and at the iron tip there appeared to be a point of fire. This he plunged into my heart several times so that it penetrated to my entrails. When he pulled it out, I felt that he took them with it, and left me utterly consumed by the great love of God. The pain was so severe that it made me utter several moans. The sweetness caused by this intense pain is so extreme that one cannot possibly wish it to cease, nor is one's soul then content with anything but God. This is not a physical, but a spiritual pain, though the body has some share in it.[9]

It should be noted that Teresa's vision was not of God but of an angel, and that she rarely saw bodily visions such as this, though

[8] *The Oxford Dictionary of the Christian Church*, 1958, p. 936.
[9] *The Life of Saint Teresa*, tr. J. M. Cohen, 1957, p. 210.

other 'visions' were apparently invisible. She received both sweetness and intense pain, but claimed that it was spiritual rather than physical. On the other hand, since the time of Freud we can hardly avoid seeing the phallic symbolism of the great spear, with the fiery point, its innermost penetration, leaving the saint utterly consumed by the love of God. Teresa would have been horrified to have a sexual interpretation placed upon her vision, but this was natural in her celibate condition, and her longings were sublimated into divine love.

Mystics often speak of raptures, or being rapt, which derives from the same root as raped. But the difference is in the consent and willing abandon to love in which the soul is female and the divinity male. Both male and female mystics generally regard the soul as female, passive and receptive, the bride of God. Eckhart said that the noblest word one could apply to the soul is 'woman', which is nobler than 'virgin'.

That the closest human relationship should be a symbol of human-divine relationship is not surprising but natural, and the use of sexual imagery in many religions may be less shocking to modern students than to Victorians. Zaehner has some valuable comments here:

> There is no point at all in blinking the fact that the raptures of the theistic mystic are closely akin to the transports of sexual union, the soul playing the part of the female and God appearing as the male. There is nothing surprising in this, for if man is made in the image of God, then it would be natural that God's love would be reflected in human love, and that the love of man for woman should reflect the love of God for the soul. . . . To drive home the close parallel between the sexual act and the mystical union with God may seem blasphemous today. Yet the blasphemy is not in the comparison, but in the degrading of the one act of which man is capable that makes him like God both in the intensity of his union with his partner and in the fact that by this union he is a co-creator with God.[10]

Reference has been made several times to the symbolism of marriage to indicate spiritual unity. This may be a marriage of divine beings, as in the extensive mythology of the Hindu god Śiva and

[10] R. C. Zaehner, *Mysticism Sacred and Profane*, pp. 151 f.

his Śakti or consort, Pārvatī, or it may be a more abstract union of complementary principles like the Chinese Yin and Yang. The Jungian school of psychology interpreted the Christian doctrine of the Trinity as a divine union which needed, however, a fourth female element which was established in the dogma of the Assumption of the Virgin Mary to place the 'eternal feminine' in the heart of the Godhead. It might have done better to consider the role of the Holy Spirit in the trinitarian unity.

The sacred marriage is not only within the divinity, but between the divine and the human. This is communal in the context of the nuptials of Yahweh with Israel in the prophecy of Hosea and in the divine wedding of the Lamb and the Church at the end of the Book of Revelation. But the mystical marriage is often individual, in which the soul is female to the male Lord. Augustine spoke of the church as 'in secret' the spouse of Christ, but proceeded to make it individual as well since it is secretly, 'in the hidden depths of the spirit, that the soul of man is joined to the word of God, so that they are two in one flesh'. The reference back is to Ephesians 5.31, where a human marriage is compared to the union of Christ with his church, but every soul may know this unity since many Christian mystics have used the image of the soul as the bride of Christ. Mother Julian said both 'God rejoices that he is our Mother', and also 'God rejoices that he is our very Spouse and our soul is his loved Wife'.

The physical union of the sexes provides an obvious parallel to the union of the soul with God, but this fits into the context of each culture and in the Christian tradition it is that of the sacred marriage, provided by the Bible itself. In India the far more erotic mythology of Krishna, against which reformers often revolted, gave new twists to the divine-human love story. Krishna not only made the milkmaids appear before him naked with hands over their heads, but he absconded with each one. They were married, but the very illegality of their amours with Krishna emphasized the priority of the divine claims above all human ties. Rādhā is often Krishna's chief paramour, yet in the eighteenth century she came to be regarded as his permanent consort and wife, and was given divine honours. Divine-human union became unity within the divinity, and this is reflected still in popular plays.

Most religions regard the sexual act as holy, and even where it is forbidden to celibate priests it is a sacrament to the laity, a holy communion in which the ministers of the sacrament are the husband and wife, who, in the Christian tradition, are to each other as Christ is to the Church. Marriage is a godlike union, and therefore adultery is universally condemned not because it is physically harmful but because it violates the divine element in mankind.

The clearest examples of sexual imagery in mysticism are found in the theistic traditions, where there is a distinction of the partners but a desire for the closest union. Monistic mysticism may be more like masturbation, pleasurable but self-centred and different from the intercourse of lovers. Reference has been made (pp. 99 f.) to the great development of erotic imagery in the cults of Krishna, an eroticism which developed away from the chaste *agapé* of the Bhagavad Gītā, and while it expressed the Krishna-Rādhā union in passionate intensity, it also produced a reaction against excess among the followers of Rāma and other groups like the Kabīris and the Sikhs.

Just as there is a strong world-denying element in Indian tradition, particularly in philosophical and ascetic circles, so there is a strong world-affirming element. This probably goes back to the Indus Valley culture, with its male and female symbolism, but it is also found in the classical Upanishads. There passages, often not quoted in anthologies, depict the Lord of Creatures creating by sexual intercourse, and giving instructions for procreation with the invocation of Vishnu and other gods.[11] In Sāmkhya and other thought it is the female Nature (Prakriti) that is active, and the Spirit or Self (Purusha) is the passive and witnessing male. The Supreme Self comes into the world by the female Māyā, creative power. In Buddhist imagery, however, the male is active Compassion, and the female is Wisdom, he is the thunderbolt and she is the lotus.

In addition to the popular Krishna-Rādhā cults, there is a very ancient tradition of Tantra, 'system' or 'rule', whose texts are largely dialogues between the god Śiva and his Śakti, active principle or female power. In contrast to world and life-negations Tantra taught that sensual energies should not be suppressed but used, for properly channelled they can bring benefit to individuals and society. Many texts speak of the coupling and creative activities of the gods, and by

[11] Brihad-āranyaka Upanishad, 6.4.

the use of imagery and sacred patterns, like mandalas, these energies can be shared. Tantric worship, particularly of the Left-hand or secret rituals, seeks the attainment of power even through normally forbidden practices: wine, meat, fish, gestures and sexual union. The Tantra texts speak of the gods, Śiva, Vishnu, Brahmā, but there is a powerful monistic current towards merging all into the female power, Śakti, of whom all other beings and powers are manifestations.[12]

Buddhism, even if originally it was a moralistic and ascetic reform, developed rapidly into religious thought and practice. Yet here there was a similar tension, between celibate monasticism, what has been called 'sexual miserliness', and forms of Tantra. The figure of Śakti is displaced, but there are personifications of Wisdom and countless images and patterns. But whereas Hindu teachers tended to see realities behind the images, Buddhists sought to empty thought of symbols, and seek for the Void or the fullness of Nirvāna.

Chinese Tao often expressed spiritual union in sexual terms, though Confucian reformers tried to check excesses. The Chinese concepts of Yin and Yang (see p. 70) are popularly identified as female and male sexual energy, but like so much in Taoism they are very complex and ambiguous. There is no Yang without Yin in it, and no Yin without Yang. The aim of discipline and art, of activity and inactivity, is harmony between the elements, and between man and the universe. The unity of Heaven and Earth was essential for ordinary life as for the prosperity of the whole of society.[13] The Taoist philosopher Chuang Tzu described the Taoist sage as having 'personal communion with the spirit of Heaven and earth' but no pride over things, he did not quarrel over right and wrong and so mixed with society, his spirit 'roamed with the creator' yet he made friends with other men, so he was profound and free, mysterious and boundless.[14]

Sexual union, then, is often used as a symbol of the union of the soul with the divine, but the way in which it is used differs according to the context of mystical doctrine. Submission to a higher power,

[12] P. Rawson, *The Art of Tantra*, 1973, pp. 15 f., 67, 183.
[13] P. Rawson and L. Legeza, *Tao*, 1973, pp. 12, 32.
[14] See W. T. de Bary, ed., *Sources of Chinese Tradition*, 1960, pp. 85 f.

and the desire to belong, can both be expressed in terms of the union of husband and wife, or of absorption into the ultimate. But a great deal of writing about sex is neither mystical nor religious, and many Tantric and Taoist techniques express only the vaguest references to the divine. On a monistic theory of mysticism perhaps this would not matter, since all is one and that includes all sexual activity. But theistic mysticism, at least, includes transcendence as well as immanence, the divine will as well as human desire, and difference as well as union. Hence orgiastic 'abodes of love' have been properly regarded as antagonistic to rather than in harmony with a mysticism which seeks union with the *divine*, the true and the holy.

Chapter 14

DRUGS AND THE OCCULT

DRUGS

G. K. Chesterton is said to have remarked that syncretism is 'religion gone to pot'. With the modern interpretation of pot as drugs, this assertion could be applied to some claims to mystical experiences. The use of drugs to obtain different states of consciousness is very ancient, and has widespread interest today. It is important therefore to consider some drug experiences and whether it is correct to give them mystical interpretations.

The use of potent drinks in sacrifice is very ancient, as hidden energy offered to gods, and as taken by the offering priests. In ancient India the god Soma was one of the most important deities, to whom many hymns of the Vedas were dedicated as a central part of the ritual. Soma was prepared from a plant which has not certainly been identified, and traditionally it was pressed, mingled with milk, and drunk on the same day. It could not have been very alcoholic in this form, and the parallel Persian drink Haoma, which is still used, has no special intoxicating properties. But it seems likely that Soma was brewed over a longer period and mixed with other ingredients, or that it may have been a different kind of drug from Haoma, more like hashish. The effects of Soma are vividly described, in terms of monistic self-glorification:

I have drunk Soma, I have become immortal.

And again:

I have passed beyond sky and earth in my glory,
have I been drinking Soma?
I will lift up the earth, and put it here or there,
have I been drinking Soma?[1]

Whatever its nature, Soma was the prerogative of the priests, and ordinary people used other drugs, alcohol, or hemp, from which the narcotic bhang has been produced in India. But it is rare to find exaltations of a drug so clearly expressed as in the hymns to the Vedic god Soma.

Another famous instance of supposed religious drug-taking was said to be found among the so-called Assassins, a name which is derived from hashish. Marco Polo said that the Sheikh of the Mountain would administer the drug when he wanted to send an emissary on a mission of murder. While the emissary slept he was introduced to the palace and on waking thought it was Paradise and so was willing to commit any deed for such a great gain. Although this story has long been widespread it is false. Hashish was known and not secret, but there is no evidence that it was used by followers of the Muslim sect to which it was applied by foreign writers. The sectaries, who were fanatical fighters, called themselves 'self-sacrificers', but the nickname Assassin is of European origin.[2]

Many kinds of drugs cause a change in consciousness and the most popular, and with some people the most respectable, is alcohol. Alcohol fairly quickly produces a feeling of confidence, expansion and enlightenment. William James said that its popularity was due to 'its power to stimulate the mystical faculties of human nature', though his definition of mysticism was vague and somewhat monistic, and he did recognize that alcoholism 'in its totality is so degrading a poisoning'.[3] Any driver knows that the effect of alcohol is to produce an unreasoning over-confidence, the cause of many accidents, and this would be dangerous ground on which to base a theory of mysticism.

William James also experimented with nitrous oxide, which he claimed stimulated 'the mystical consciousness in an extraordinary

[1] Rig Veda, 8.48; 10.119. [2] B. Lewis, *The Assassins*, 1967, pp. 12 f.
[3] William James, *The Varieties of Religious Experience*, 1902, ch. XVI.

degree. Depth beyond depth of truth seems revealed to the inhaler.' But this truth escaped on return to normal consciousness, and if any words remained over they were 'the veriest nonsense'.

In recent years great claims have been made for the drug mescalin, made known to a wide audience by the novelist Aldous Huxley in experiments conducted in 1954 and described in his book *The Doors of Perception*. Mescalin is prepared from a root called peyotl, which is used in Mexico and the southern parts of the United States. Huxley says that mescalin is better than hashish, opium or alcohol in that it is 'less toxic', but in suitable doses 'it changes the quality of consciousness more profoundly'.[4] Mescalin leaves no hangover and apparently does not become an addiction, though it is hard to see why not if the effects are as satisfactory as is claimed. Huxley does not tell us that mescalin is used clinically to produce a state similar to that of schizophrenia.

Huxley took his pill of mescalin sitting in his study facing a vase of flowers. After half an hour they became transfigured and he claimed that they gave him mystical vision.

I continued to look at the flowers, and in their living light I seemed to detect the qualitative equivalent of breathing—but of a breathing without returns to a starting-point, with no recurrent ebbs but only a repeated flow from beauty to heightened beauty, from deeper to ever deeper meaning. Words like Grace and Transfiguration came into my mind, and this of course was what, among other things, they stood for. My eyes travelled from the rose to the carnation, and from that feathery incandescence to the smooth scrolls of sentient amethyst which were the iris. The Beatific Vision, *Sat Chit Ananda*, Being-Awareness-Bliss—for the first time I understood, not on the verbal level, not by inchoate hints or at a distance, but precisely and completely what those prodigious syllables referred to.[5]

Huxley's attention was then drawn to a chair in the room, which also shone with inner light.

[4] Aldous Huxley, *The Doors of Perception*, pp. 15 f.
[5] Ibid., pp. 12 f.

The legs, for example, of that chair—how miraculous their tubularity, how supernatural was their polished smoothness! I spent several minutes—or was it several centuries?—not merely gazing at those bamboo legs, but actually *being* them—or rather being myself in them; or, to be still more accurate . . . being my Not-self in the Not-self which was the chair.

Next he turned to the trousers on his own legs.

Those folds in the trousers—what a labyrinth of endlessly significant complexity! And the texture of the grey flannel—how rich, how deeply, mysteriously sumptuous! . . . the folds of my grey flannels were charged with 'is-ness'.

Yet while fascinated by these material objects, and thinking to perceive their inner meaning and infinite value, Huxley did not find the same in human beings. His wife and a great friend were in the room, but 'both belonged to the world from which, for the moment, mescalin had delivered me—the world of selves, of time, of moral judgements and utilitarian considerations', and these other selves were 'enormously irrelevant'.

Huxley's account of his experience is remarkable from several points of view. He had already written on religions and philosophies, yet now he says that before taking mescalin he had 'known contemplation only in its humbler, its more ordinary forms'. What he had written, therefore, of God, the Absolute, or the Buddha-nature had been simply intellectual, book-learning, with virtually no religious experience. But now he claims that by the use of a drug he has a vision of God, the Beatific Vision, which is the goal of Christian mystical striving. But he gives no account of it, and it would be rash to take his word at its face value. Huxley equates the Beatific Vision of the Christian mystic with the Absolute of Hindu philosophy, which is denoted by Being-Awareness-Bliss, and also with the Body of the Buddha which, he says, in the words of some Zen Buddhists 'was the hedge at the bottom of the garden'. But the confusion of thought, and the incongruous accounts given by Huxley, provide a real danger that the deeper matters with which he claimed to deal could be dismissed as nonsense. Far from being adopted to relieve the tedium of ordinary church services, by doses of mescalin as he suggested, the large claims of mysticism, if this is it, risk being dismissed out of hand.)

It was the publication of Huxley's book which stimulated Zaehner to write his important *Mysticism Sacred and Profane*, for he says that he doubts whether he would have been rash enough to enter the field of comparative mysticism, but 'Huxley left us no choice'. Zaehner did not simply write but took mescalin himself, with almost opposite results to Huxley. His experiments were conducted in Oxford, under the direction of a doctor. Like Huxley, his sensations of colour were intensified by the drug, but he disliked them, and even the apparent expansion and contraction of a rose window in Christ Church cathedral he found 'irritating'. Later looking at a picture of the Adoration of the Magi, he found it 'wildly amusing' and broke into uncontrollable laughter. The sight of a Persian rug produced the same effect. Zaehner's conclusion was that the experience was trivial, though it seemed hilariously funny. He felt that it was even 'anti-religious', in the sense that it did not conform to religious experience and, rather to his disappointment, the drug did not produce any kind of 'natural mystical experience'.[6]

W. T. Stace has also written on drug experience and much more favourably, remarking, 'It's not a matter of its being *similar* to mystical experience; it *is* mystical experience.' On which Zaehner comments that Stace could have no conception of 'the *interreligious* dimension of the problem', meaning basically the differences between theistic and monistic and naturalistic forms of mysticism.[7]

In 1962 an experiment was conducted for a Harvard thesis, based on Stace's 'typology of mysticism', to which reference was made earlier (pp. 11 f.). Twenty young Protestant graduates listened to a Good Friday service, while half of them received a drug similar to LSD and half did not. Then their 'scores' of feeling on the Stace typology were listed: on unity, transcendence, bliss, ineffability, and so on. The scores of those who had not received the drug were sensationally lower, as might have been expected. But the published results of the experiment tell us little of the *religious* experience

[6] R. C. Zaehner, *Mysticism Sacred and Profane*, pp. 212 f.
[7] R. C. Zaehner, *Drugs, Mysticism and Make-believe*, 1972, pp. 79, 88 f., 103 f.

of these guinea-pigs. Was their understanding of the events of Good Friday increased or diminished in meditation, and was it better with or without drugs? We do not know, but we might guess.

This experiment was called a 'miracle' by Timothy Leary, the 'high priest of LSD' in the sixties. His own reactions after eating some of the Mexican sacred mushrooms were described as 'the deepest religious experience of my life'. Leary held that 'the instruments of systematic religion are chemicals. Drugs. Dope. If you are serious about your religion, if you really wish to commit yourself to the spiritual quest, you must learn how to use psycho-chemicals. Drugs are the religion of the twenty-first century.' Further, 'LSD is Western yoga. The aim of all Eastern religion, like the aim of LSD, is basically to get high: that is, to expand your consciousness and find ecstasy and revelation within.'[8]

One should not generalize about 'all Eastern religion' for it has many varieties, as readers of this book will know. Christianity, Islam and Judaism are Eastern religions and indeed all the world's great living religions began in Asia. Even if attention is confined to Indian religion, there are many important differences. Buddhism, for example, does not seek 'to expand consciousness' but to get rid of it, in the indescribable Void or Nirvāna. There are strong currents of asceticism and sexual denial in Indian religion, as well as the reverse. But according to Leary, 'The three inevitable goals of the LSD session are to discover and make love with God, to discover and make love with yourself, and to discover and make love with a woman.'[9]

Leary was at least more open than some prudish or prudent drug-takers in claiming that LSD is 'the most powerful aphrodisiac', and if his experiences were mystical he would be a world-affirming nature mystic. But he toys with pantheistic monism, exhorting his followers to 'be God and the universe', and affirming, 'I am God of light. Who am I? I'm you.'[10] It is not clear now whether Leary retains any of these views, since his imprisonment, escape and further arrest, for he was said in 1974 to have denounced psychedelic drugs and informed on illegal traffickers. From his writings it appears that the

[8] Timothy Leary, *The Politics of Ecstasy*, Paladin ed., 1970, pp. 13, 38, 112 f.
[9] Ibid., p. 107. [10] Ibid., pp. 290, 31.

DRUGS AND THE OCCULT

use of drugs is self-defeating. Most of them are addictive, so that claims that drugs give a sense of freedom are illusory for if one depends upon a drug then one is not free. Further, drugs are too physically centred, and they give no help against old age and death. But mystics often claim a deepening and strengthening of mystical experience with advancing years, and all religions believe in life after death.

Claimed as more significant than the amateurish efforts of Leary and Huxley were the experiments of an American anthropologist in Mexico, Carlos Castaneda. For five years he took drugs, mescalin and others, under the direction of a Yaqui Indian, Don Juan. Castaneda had terrifying experiences, seeming to meet spirits, huge animals, and death itself. The god of the drug, Mescalito, was only rarely encountered and after long preparation. Eventually Castaneda saw Mescalito, like a man but 'his eyes were the water I had just seen! They had the same enormous volume, the sparkling of gold and black. His head was pointed like a strawberry; his skin was green, dotted with innumerable warts. Except for the pointed shape, his head was exactly like the surface of the peyote plant.' Castaneda collapsed and knelt before the god, telling all about his life and fearing that death had come. In a hole in the back of the god's hand he saw himself as an old man with sparks flying round him until he disappeared. Mescalito looked at him deeply, turned away, hopped like a cricket, and was gone.[11]

Castaneda's visions read like nightmares, with fantastic apparitions as might be expected from drugs, and rarely is there anything that might be called mystical from a religious standpoint. Finally, after a night of terror which threatened his sanity and life itself, he gave up his apprenticeship to Don Juan, confessing that 'I was not, nor will I ever be, prepared to undergo the rigours of such a training'. There is no easy road to mystical experience here, and no suggestion that drugs can replace or supplement religion.

OCCULT AND ESOTERIC

The popularity of drugs in the sixties may be fading now, but interest

[11] C. Castaneda, *The Teachings of Don Juan*, Penguin edn, 1970, pp. 99 f.

in the occult seems perennial in different forms, and for many people the occult is mystical. Both drugs and the occult may seem to offer more reality, more personal experience, than either everyday life or formal religion. Leary and others attacked the money-based 'work culture' of our time for its materialism, and by offering experiences of mystical oneness through drugs or yoga, Zen or transcendental meditation, they made a great appeal to young and old.

The revival of occultism in our time seems to be a reversal of its decline from the eighteenth century onwards. Rationalism has failed to satisfy spiritual needs, and it appears that science has inadequate answers for the uncertainties and despairs of the industrial age. Drugs have awakened interest in the expansion of experience, and many oriental Gurus offer methods of training that must make church leaders wonder why they set their demands so low. All kinds of superstitions abound, and it may be that superstition lingers, or revives, when formal religion declines. Belief in phenomena such as Unidentified Flying Objects may provide a supernatural element to drab lives, as Jung suggested. Astrology has countless followers and semi-believers, and a UNESCO inquiry in 1973 reported that 50 per cent of newspapers in Britain, France, Belgium, Switzerland and U.S.A. had daily astrological columns, and employed thousands of advisers.

Perhaps the most remarkable is the revival of belief in witchcraft. Discredited from the seventeenth century onwards, and thought to be extinct except among the most ignorant and illiterate by the nineteenth, there are today many witches' covens, which claim to be perpetuating an ancient religion which had been temporarily repressed by Christianity. It is very doubtful whether such claims can be proved, and there are probably no historical connections between medieval covens, themselves largely the creation of the fantasies and repressions of the inquisitors, and modern groups. There is no reason why people should not form societies and dress or undress in rituals, or dance naked in the woods, provided that they do not offend society or harm enemies or deviant members. But that witchcraft societies, or other occult groups, are properly mystical may be debated. Witch leaders sometimes claim to be infused with the Life Force, or the Spirit of the Universe, a claim that ancient witches never made and which owes more to Bernard Shaw or Henri Bergson than to witch history.

If there is anything mystical in witchcraft or astrological or other occult beliefs, it is probably a naturalistic pantheism. There is no reason to doubt the sincerity of claims to spiritual experience, but the pity is that so much seems to be confused and often self-contradictory, and that more systematic forms of mystical practice are not followed. There is no need to deny that there are parallels between some drug or occult experiences and some elements in religious mysticism. The experience of harmony with the universe is fairly common, though it generally looks at the brighter side of the world and neglects the suffering and evil that affect much of human life. It is a common criticism of mysticism in general that it is too optimistic, or self-centred, though some of the great mystics past and present have been active in the world, and one might instance Pope John XXIII and Mother Teresa of Calcutta.

There is a natural reaction among religious people to suggestions that drugs or occult practices can provide experiences comparable with those of the great mystics. But comparability is not the same as identity, and mystics have generally taught that there are various stages on the path, from purgation from sin to the vision of God. The trouble nowadays is that there is much confusion generated by the notion that drug experience is the *same* as the mystical vision of God. Ideas of a world Force, an Absolute, or a Void are identified with belief in the personal God in whom theistic mystics believe. It has been well remarked that both doctrine and experience have been misinterpreted by those writers who identify them as all the same. 'To at least some extent the responsibility of this seduction of the innocent must lie with such authors as Huxley, Alan Watts, and others who in their various writings imposed upon the psychedelic experience essentially Eastern ideas and terminology which a great many persons then assumed to be the sole and accurate way of approaching and interpreting such experience.'[12]

Even within one tradition mystics do not speak the same language

[12] R. E. L. Masters and J. Houston, *The Varieties of Psychedelic Experience*, 1966, p. 260. See Alan Watts, *The Way of Zen, Beyond Theology*, etc.

or transmit the same message. Hindu philosophy was deeply divided between the monism of Śankara and the modified non-dualism of Rāmānuja, and even more by the personal theism of the *bhakta* devotees. Muslim teachers like Junayd and Ibn 'Arabī differed widely, as the sin-obsessed Augustine differed from the world-affirming Thomas Traherne. But theistic mystics unite in believing that their experiences are not their own invention, they are the gift of God. They may be helped by physical aids, but they depend for their origination and their consummation on the God 'of whom, and through whom, and unto whom, are all things'.

Chapter 15

MYSTICISM AND
RELIGIOUS EXPERIENCE

ORDINARY AND EXPERT

'This mystical way of looking at things', says the philosopher J. N. Findlay, 'enters into the experience of most men at many times'. Rather than being a peculiar practice, possibly heretical, mysticism is but the fullest extension of the common way of humanity. On this view, 'the so-called great mystics, people like Plotinus, Jalalu'din Rumi, St Teresa and so on, are merely people who carry to the point of genius an absolutely normal, ordinary, indispensable side of human experience'.[1]

Such statements would not have been accepted by many writers on mysticism in the past, and mystics have often been regarded not simply as experts in a field in which we are all engaged, but as a class quite apart. Yet there may be historical reasons for this separation of mystics away from the rest of us. Certainly in the Bible, or at least in the New Testament, if any of its teachings can be claimed as mystical, there is no differentiation between two classes of believers, or any suggestion that union with God is closed to most followers of the Way. According to the Fourth Gospel Jesus told his disciples to 'abide in me and I in you', but there is no indication that this undoubtedly mystical union was to be confined to the twelve apostles or their successors in office. The doctrine of the 'priesthood of all believers' would preclude such a restriction. The same Gospel

[1] J. N. Findlay, *Ascent to the Absolute*, p. 164. For Jalalu'din Rūmī see pp. 135–6 above.

185

affirms that it was publicly in the temple that Jesus cried, 'If any man thirst let him come to me and drink', and 'From him shall flow rivers of living water'. Similarly Paul wrote of 'this mystery among the Gentiles, which is Christ in you', and he exhorted all his converts to 'walk in him, rooted and builded up in him' (Col. 1.27; 2.6 f.).

But it appears that when Christian teachers began more fully to adopt the language of the Greek mysteries, which were reserved for the initiate and different from the religion of the common people, there came into Christian language some differentiation not only between Christians and the pagan world, but between the experts and ordinary believers. Clement of Alexandria spoke of normal faith as 'suitable for people who are in a hurry', but knowledge (*gnosis*) had been given to 'initiate' developed souls into the higher 'mysteries'. Ordinary Christians received the 'lesser mysteries', but Gnosis led the initiates into the 'great mysteries'. Origen followed this distinction between faith and knowledge, speaking rather arrogantly of the 'popular, irrational faith' which led to physical 'somatic Christianity', whereas Gnosis led to a 'spiritual Christianity' which looked for eternal truths and was not tied to the mere details of the Gospel stories which so appealed to the masses.

The second-century teachers accepted the current Greek view that it was 'not lawful to reveal the mysteries to profane persons', and thus they helped to promote the notion that mystical experience was beyond and different from primary Christian experience. Then the persecution of the church in different periods of the early centuries encouraged the separation of believers from the world, and fostered the notion that Christianity was a secret cult like the mystery religions. Finally, the development of the hermit and monastic movements, whether single recluses or ascetic communities, further encouraged the separation of the spiritual athlete from the mundane Christian and this process was accentuated when Christianity became tolerated and then the official religion of the state. As in other ascetic movements, no doubt ordinary believers thought that it was an advantage to have holy men living near them who would bring additional blessings to their locality. Yet it was the help provided by the proletariat which enabled ascetics to survive, and, as Buddhist texts had admitted centuries before in a revealing phrase, the monks ensured that their place of retreat had 'a village nearby for support'.

Mystical writers, at least from Gregory I onwards, distinguished two kinds of Christian life, the active and the contemplative. In the fourteenth century Walter Hilton said that 'the active life lies in love and charity showed outwardly by good bodily works; in fulfilling God's commandments and the seven works of mercy', and 'this life belongs to all worldly men who have riches and plenty of goods to spend', though much of it may include fastings and other penances. But contemplative life 'belongs specially to those who for love of God forsake all worldly riches, honour and outward business, and wholly give themselves body and soul, with might and power, to the service of God by spiritual occupation'. And the *Cloud of Unknowing* declares roundly that the active life is lower and the contemplative is higher, and a man may not be fully contemplative if he is in part active.[2]

Most medieval Christian mystical writers were monks or nuns, or clergy, all of them separate from the ordinary occupations of their fellow-Christians and only too apt to consider, and be considered by the laity, that they lived closer to God than those who were involved in family life. Such an opinion could have had no basis in the Gospels, where both priests and scribes are severely censured, and in the Middle Ages also there were frequent criticisms of monks for the unholiness of their lives. An Indian text remarks that 'a Brahmin learned in the Vedas' is one of the lewdest beings, and Boccaccio at least would have applied a similar judgement to monks and nuns alike. Nevertheless, monks claimed that their life was superior to that of their 'even-Christians'.

There were, however, noted lay men and women living in the world yet famed for their mystical devotions and writings. Catharine of Genoa in the fifteenth century was a favourite example, being suddenly converted after ten years of marriage, though finding a worldly life burdensome until her husband was also converted. He became a Franciscan tertiary but Catharine joined no order, and they both worked for the care of the sick in hospital. At the same time Catharine had visions and mystical experiences, and her spiritual doctrines were published in her autobiography and in dialogues of 'the Soul and the Body'.

In the countries of the Reformation the separation between active

[2] *The Scale of Perfection*, pp. 2 f.; *The Cloud of Unknowing*, p. 66.

and contemplative largely disappeared, though the clergy remained a class apart and, being more literate than their neighbours, the priests and pastors continued to compose the majority of devotional and mystical works. But with the growth of lay participation and general literacy the laity had much easier access to mystical writings. Mystical experiences might come to men irrespective of the social class, but a wider awareness of mystical teachings in different traditions is a special feature of our own times. If, as we have maintained, there is Protestant mysticism, then it has abandoned the distinction that had been made between mystical and ordinary religious experience. And if there is Nature mysticism, whether theistic or pantheistic does not matter for the moment, then such mysticism is available to everybody and not to a special class. There are still experts, recipients of special revelations or intuitions, but they are only different in degree from their fellow-believers who should also be capable of receiving divine aid and communion.

A curious variation on the distinction of expert from ordinary may be seen in the attempts of some sociologists to explain mystical phenomena as the product of special social conditions, with the assumption that mysticism would disappear if conditions improved. Karl Marx spoke of religion as 'the cry of the oppressed creature, the heart of a heartless world, the drug of the masses'. An Italian writer has seen more mysticism in 'religions of the oppressed' than in more stable classes and societies. And the anthropologist I. M. Lewis speaks of mysticism as 'an attempt to enrich the spiritual armoury of a community beset by chronic environmental uncertainty, or rapid and inexplicable social change'.[3] Hence mystical experience would seem to be favoured, if not completely generated, by disorder, repression, denial of political expression, the deprived status of women, and so on. There would appear to be waves of mystical fervour, corresponding to external pressures. Yet Lewis agrees that there is an 'ever-present need for mystical excitement and drama', and although an agnostic himself he accepts that 'we live in an age of marginal mystical recrudescence, a world where Humanists seem positively archaic'.

On the other hand, E. O'Brien, an American theologian, in a

[3] I. M. Lewis, *Ecstatic Religion*, pp. 20, 203 f.

survey chiefly of Christian mysticism, stresses the spontaneity and involuntariness of mystical experiences. These are normally contrary to the subject's theological position, so that they are challenging and demanding. The experience is self-authenticating, and needs no external authority. It follows that mystical experience occurs in all ages, almost irrespective of external circumstances. O'Brien considers that apparent variety in the mystical outputs in different ages is illusory, for experience occurs whether time and place a.e favourable or not. It merely happens that more attention is paid to it in some ages and therefore better records have been kept when it is fashionable than when it is not. As a theologian he would agree that mystical experiences are of divine origin and not dependent on social conditions.[4]

I. M. Lewis considers that O'Brien's theory would 'almost close the door to sociological analysis', and not unnaturally from his own viewpoint regards this as a 'stultifying conclusion'. Yet he himself maintains the universality of mystical experience, 'at some stage in its history'.[5] The truth is probably somewhere between these two points of view. Social conditions, such as persecution, may affect the extent of expression of religion, though not always to its detriment. Yet degrees of literacy may make it difficult to estimate the circulation of mystical writing in any one time. Theologically it has long been recognized that there are periods when it seems that the Lord does not speak, either by prophets or by more mystical ways. Mystics have recognized times of spiritual dryness and 'dark nights of the soul', but since God is eternal and unchanging he will speak again in his own good time.

MYSTICAL AND RELIGIOUS

'I believe that mysticism enters into almost everyone's attitudes, and that it is as much a universal background to experience as the open sky is to vision: to ignore it is to be drearily myopic, and to take the splendour and depth out of everything.' Findlay justifies his statement by comparisons from art, music and mathematics. Some

[4] E. O'Brien, *Varieties of Mystic Experience*, 1965.
[5] I. M. Lewis, *Ecstatic Religion*, pp. 24 f., 18.

people are colour-blind, some are tone-deaf, and others have an aversion to mathematics, but that does not show that these things do not exist. 'Some people refuse to cultivate mystical ways of looking at things, and in fact resolutely exclude them. . . . This kind of experiential and logical myopia only shows that there are many myopic people, and that some are deliberately myopic: it shows nothing about the logical or illogical character of mystical utterances and experiences.'[6]

The view of mysticism which Findlay expounds is one which seeks a unity at the centre of things, that alone guarantees the coherence which is necessary to all rational enterprises. Unmystical ways of looking at the world see it as made up of separate facts and features, which it is difficult to relate to any general structure. A popular view of science imagines that it is simply concerned with the collection of facts; 'Facts alone are wanted in life', in the words of Mr Gradgrind of *Hard Times*. But great scientists, like great artists, seek the unity behind diversity, and from the coherence of their own inner life come to understand and have communion with others. Neville Cardus, the great music and cricket expositor, said that music is not a series of propositions, but 'when we listen to music, if we listen properly, we take part in a co-union; we taste the body of genius, enter into the mind of the man. . . . If I know that my Redeemer liveth it is not on the Church's testimony but because of what Handel affirms'.[7]

Findlay's 'logic of mysticism' is monistic in that it is 'oriented towards an absolute: the feature of absolute unity because an absolute is necessarily single and unique'. It treats the 'identity of everything, including oneself, with the absolute' as a vivid personal experience, which may lead on to ecstasy. We have seen that monism is one of the most important forms of mysticism, though not the only one, and religiously there seems to be a constant need for a more personal and theistic form of mystical relationship. Findlay recognizes that many states of being may exist between the extreme alienation which often appears in this world, and the ultimate which is 'the extreme of unity', but clearly there is tension between a

[6] J. N. Findlay, *The Ascent to the Absolute*, pp. 182, 164.
[7] Quoted in *The Guardian*, 4 April 1975.

philosophical theory of absolute monism and the loving relationships of popular religion.

For a long time we have been assuming that there is a connection between mysticism and ordinary religious experience and something further must be said in conclusion. Religion means many things, and some modern writers use it in the sense of outward forms and practices which are often little more than religiosity. But religion is derived from *religio* as a non-material bond, and ultimately as the bond of the divine and the human. Even the most transcendentalist religions believe in the communication of the divine will to man and in the duty of man to conform to this revelation. It has been seen that neither in the Old Testament nor in the Qur'ān is there an unbridgeable 'gulf' between God and man, and that both contain accounts of the divine presence and of communion with God. Even the Calvinist Jonathan Edwards spoke of his aim as 'to be with God, and to spend my eternity in divine love, and holy communion with Christ'.

The religious experience of the ordinary believer is often spoken of as 'communion' with God, and this is one of the commonest Christian expressions in the blessing given by Paul to the Corinthians: 'The communion of the Holy Spirit be with you all.'[8] It may be said that 'communion' is not the same as 'union', but it is not basically different. 'Comm-union' means 'union with', and in religious usage the difference between communion and union can be claimed as a matter of degree. Hence the religious experience of the ordinary believer is in the same class as that of the mystic, the difference is one of degree but not of kind. The mystic, as Findlay says, simply carries to the point of genius that which is the ordinary and indispensable side of religious experience. That the ordinary believer seeks communion with God is witnessed by countless hymns and devotional writings, Christian and Hindu, Muslim and Buddhist. That there are spiritual experts or athletes in all these religions is obvious, but even where they have separated themselves

[8] 2 Corinthians 13.13. The Greek (*koinovia*) is translated 'fellowship in the Holy Spirit' in the New English Bible, and 'sharing of the Spirit' in Philippians 2.1. The sense is that of communion with God and man.

off from their fellows in monasteries or caves, they have depended upon the common folk who saw in them the expression of their own deepest needs.

The important distinctions in mysticism are not so much between the layman and the expert as between the assumptions and the objects of the mystical quest. It is popularly said that all religions are the same though their differences should be evident to unprejudiced eyes and part of their fascination is their diversity. Similarly it is held that mysticism is one and the same everywhere, whatever the religious environment may be, and indeed that mystical experiences are the uniting bond between religions that profess very different doctrines. Thus Stace claims that 'the Christian experience is basically the same as that which is described in the Māndukya Upanishad'.[9] This most monistic of the Upanishads declares that the fourth state, beyond waking, dreaming and dreamless sleep, is the knowledge of the Self. Comparing this with a statement by the medieval Catholic mystic Ruysbroeck, who spoke of finding 'an Eternal Light' within, Stace comments that it is 'identical point by point', 'except that the mystical experience is interpreted theistically as a seeing of God'. But what an exception this is! It is like telling a lover that his experience of embracing his beloved is the same as embracing the hedge at the bottom of the garden. The whole difference that Buber makes between the relations of I-Thou and I-It is here, and it is useless to claim that the experience of unity is all that matters, irrespective of the object, since the object makes all the difference. In fact for the theistic believer God is not the object but the subject, the initiator of the experience, which he gives by grace. This theistic claim is often underestimated or ignored, but it is fundamental and deserves proper study as evidence.

However, there may be a close similarity or even identity between natural and monistic mysticism, what Zaehner called pan-en-henic and pantheistic. Nature mystics claim experiences of oneness with the world, and Huxley even felt that he *was* the legs of a chair, and this was experience of the Absolute, of Being-Awareness-Bliss.[10]

[9] W. T. Stace, *Mysticism and Philosophy*, pp. 100, 88, 94. Māndukya Upanishad, 12.
[10] See above, p. 178.

Allowing for poetical exaggeration, there does seem to have been a feeling of oneness with everything, and it is similar to the Upanishadic statements, 'Thou art That', or 'I am Brahman'. It is true that the Indian monists have tended to regard the world as absolutely non-existent, though the Upanishads do not say this, and this would be at variance with the nature mystic's delight in the world, with its hills and trees, sun and flowers. But both the unworldly monism and the natural pan-en-henism are 'all-in-one-ism', for both claim to experience a unity without any differentiation. Huxley actually being the chair legs was, as he saw, similar to the non-dualist being Brahman.

Indian monists are often called pantheists, and they as often object to this name. They teach *a-dvaita*, non-duality, not-two-ness, and not only affirm that the soul must enter into union with the Absolute, but realize that it is the Absolute and that nothing else exists. This is pure identity, not God, and nothing can be said of it except 'Not this, not this'. If it is not God, it is not pan-*theism*, and it might as well be equivalent to the world, to everything, or to nothing.

Negations may suit some philosophers but there have been constant reactions against them among religious people, and even nature mystics are rarely content with mere oneness and seek for the 'Spirit that impels all thinking things'. The theistic mystical experience is different from pantheist or pan-en-henic because it seeks a union with God in a relation of love. There can hardly be love for the negative Absolute or for chair legs, since love requires personal relations and some difference of subject and object. Theistic mystics have spoken of being lost in God, or melted away in love for him, but some distinctness of the soul must remain in order to have the experience of divine love. Even where theistic mystics have spoken, occasionally, of being divinized or deified this is a transformation but not an annihilation. The soul may be regarded as part of the body of God, or permeated with the divine substance, but distinctions and differences remain to enable the divine love to be experienced.

Between the different traditions of theistic or personalistic mysticism there are distinctions again. The bhakta of Krishna would hold that his passionate love for the divine cowherd is different from adoration of the gracious Amida Buddha, and Christian devotion to Christ crucified differs from the Sufi's search for the one true Light. Perhaps to the extent that Sufism and some forms of Buddhism have less clearly defined divine objects they may have tended to slip into the Void or into monism. In Christian mysticism the complexity of belief in the Trinity has ensured the maintenance of doctrines of transcendence and immanence, and of loving union with Christ. Although some Christian mystics have spoken in impersonal terms, Christ has remained central to Christian mysticism and forms its distinctive element.

In modern times mysticism may seem to have declined in the churches, though it was never confined to formal organizations. The mystical hymns of Charles Wesley are perhaps less sung today than fifty years ago, being displaced by thin and ephemeral compositions. The current stress on social works in Christianity has been decried as a diversion from true religion, but there is a mysticism of social concern and many mystics have been practical people. More damaging to Christian spirituality has been an excessive pre-occupation with organization and the validity of orders, on the one hand, and on the other the attempts of theologians to debunk the Gospels and kill off God. Perhaps it is true, as Findlay suggests, that orthodox theology is too intent on considering the properties, or non-existence, of the deity without giving time to mystical experience.

Meanwhile 'the hungry sheep look up and are not fed'. For whatever else may be said about the present generation, if it is not church-going neither is it irreligious. In some ways there is a boom in religion, in mysticism, and even in the occult. A century ago many eminent Victorians, Marx and Bradlaugh, and perhaps Huxley and Darwin, were anticipating the collapse of religion by the end of the century. How astonished and incredulous they would be to see religious musicals and dramas playing to packed houses of educated young people in our great cities today. Further, the wide and constantly increasing popularity of the comparative study of religions, which in my college has doubled its numbers in successive years, is proof of the constant appeal of religion and of the search for something deeper than arid non-theology.

Greater than compromise structures and agreed formulas is

spiritual experience, and the mystical needs of human beings are so urgent that they will seek their satisfaction wherever it may be found. Or, in a more theological interpretation, the divine Spirit is seeking man, and will not be restricted to forms or theories. If the churches are emptying today the cellars are filling, with men and women engaged on the mystical understanding of their own natures and intent on communion and union with the divine.

Select
Bibliography

———

Index

SELECT BIBLIOGRAPHY

The literature of mysticism is immense and reference is made here only to works that are quoted or mentioned in the text.

Abdel-Kader, A. H., *The Life, Personality and Writings of al-Junayd*. Luzac 1962.
Achārānga Sūtra, in *Jaina Sūtras*, tr. H. Jacobi, Oxford 1884.
Allchin, F. R., tr., *Kavitāvalī*. Allen & Unwin 1964.
Arberry, A. J., *The Romance of the Rubáiyát*. Allen & Unwin 1959.
Archer, J. C., *The Mystical Elements in Muhammad*. New Haven 1924.
Baëta, C. G., *Prophetism in Ghana*. S.C.M. 1962.
Barth, K., *Church Dogmatics*, tr. G. T. Thomson, Clark 1936.
Bary, W. T. de, ed., *Sources of Chinese Tradition*. Columbia 1960.
Bastide, R., *African Civilisations in the New World*. E. T. Hurst 1971.
Bhagavad Gita: A Verse Translation, G. Parrinder. Sheldon 1974.
Bhagavad-Gītā, with the Commentary of Śrī Śankarachāryā, tr. A. M. Sāstri, Madras 1897.
Bhaktivedanta, A. C., *Bhagavad-gītā As It Is*. Collier 1972.
Bhattacharya, D., *Love Songs of Chandidās*. Allen & Unwin 1967.
Bhattacharya, D., *Love Songs of Vidyāpati*. Allen & Unwin 1963.
Blakney, R. B., *Meister Eckhart*. Harper 1941.
Blofeld, J., *Beyond the Gods*. Allen & Unwin 1974.
Brandel-Syrier, M., *Black Woman in Search of God*. Lutterworth 1962.

Brihad-āranyaka, see *Upanishads*.

Buber, M., *Between Man and Man*, tr. T. and T. Clark 1947.

Buber, M., *I and Thou*, tr. 1937.

Castaneda, C., *The Teachings of Don Juan*. Penguin 1970.

Chan, W. T., *A Source Book in Chinese Philosophy*. Princeton 1963.

Chāndogya, see *Upanishads*.

Chuang Tzu, see W. T. de Bary.

Cloud of Unknowing, ed., E. Underhill. Watkins 1946.

Cohen, A., *Everyman's Talmud*. Dent 1949 edn.

Cohen, J. M., *The Life of Saint Teresa*. Penguin 1957.

Coleridge, S. T., *Dejection*, 1802.

Conze, E., *Buddhist Texts*, ed., Cassirer 1954.

Conze, E., *Buddhist Thought in India*, Allen & Unwin 1962.

Cragg, K., *The Event of the Qur'ān*. Allen & Unwin 1971.

Cragg, K., *The Mind of the Qur'ān*. Allen & Unwin 1973.

Cross, F. L., ed., *The Oxford Dictionary of the Christian Church*. Oxford 1958.

Devanandan, P. D., *The Concept of Māyā*. Y.M.C.A. Calcutta 1950.

Dhavamony, M., *Love of God according to Śaiva Siddhānta*. Oxford 1971.

Dīgha Nikāya, tr. T. W. Rhys Davids in *Dialogues of the Buddha*. Luzac 1899.

Dionysius, *Mystical Theology*, tr. Shrine of Wisdom. 1923.

Dumont, P. E., tr., *L'Īśvaragītā*. Baltimore & Paris 1933.

Eliade, M., *Shamanism*, tr. Routledge 1964.

Eliade, M., *Yoga, Immortality and Freedom*. tr. Routledge 1958.

Epstein, I., *Judaism*. Penguin 1959.

Field, M. J., *Religion and Medicine of the Gã People*, Oxford 1937.

Field, M. J., *Search for Security*. Faber 1960.

Findlay, J. N., *Ascent to the Absolute*. Allen & Unwin 1970.

Fremantle, A., *The Protestant Mystics*. Mentor 1965.

Ganadharavāda, tr. M. P. Vijaya, Ahmedabad 1950.

Ghose, Aurobindo, *The Ideal of Human Unity*. Pondicherry 1919.

Ghose, Aurobindo, *The Synthesis of Yoga*. Pondicherry 1948.

Gombrich, R. F., *Precept and Practice*. Oxford 1971.

Grierson, G. and Barnett, L. D., tr., *Lallā-Vākyāni*. Royal Asiatic Society 1920.

SELECT BIBLIOGRAPHY

Guillaume, A., tr., *The Life of Muhammad*. Oxford 1955.

Hardy, F., 'Mādhavêndra Purī' in *Journal of the Royal Asiatic Society* 1974.

Hill, W. D. P., tr., *The Bhagavadgītā*. Oxford 1928.

Hill, W. D. P., *The Holy Lake of the Acts of Rāma*. Oxford 1952.

Hilton, W., *The Scale of Perfection*, modernized edn. Burns Oates 1927.

Hooper, J. S. M., *Hymns of the Ālvārs*. Oxford 1929.

Hudson, W. H., *Far Away and Long Ago*. Dent 1939.

Huxley, A., *The Doors of Perception*. Chatto 1954.

Jacobs, L., *Hasidic Prayer*. Routledge 1972.

James, W., *The Varieties of Religious Experience*. 1902, Longmans 1929.

John of the Cross, *Poems*, tr. A. Peers. Burns Oates 1947.

Julian, Mother, *Revelations of Divine Love*, ed. G. Warrack. Methuen 1934.

Jung, C. G., *Memories, Dreams, Reflections*, tr. Fontana 1967.

Kern, H., tr., *Saddharma-Pundarīka or The Lotus of the True Law*. Oxford 1909.

Keyt, G., tr., *Gīta Govinda*. Bombay 1947.

Klostermaier, K., *Hindu and Christian in Vrindaban*. S.C.M. 1969.

Landau, R., *The Philosophy of Ibn 'Arabī*. Allen & Unwin 1959.

Laski, M., *Ecstasy*. Cresset 1961.

Leary, T., *The Politics of Ecstasy*. Paladin 1970 edn.

Lewis, B., *The Assassins*. Weidenfeld 1967.

Lewis, I. M., *Ecstatic Religion*. Penguin 1971.

Lossky, V., *The Mystical Theology of the Eastern Church*, tr. Clarke 1957.

Lotus Sūtra, see Kern.

Mahā-Saccaka Sutta, in *Middle Length Sayings*, tr. I. B. Horner. Luzac 1954.

Massignon, L., *Essai sur les Origines du Lexique technique de la Mystique Musulmane*. Vrin, Paris 1954.

Massignon, L., *Le Dīwān d'al-Hallāj*. Geuthner, Paris 1955.

Masters, R. E. L. and Houston, J., *The Varieties of Psychedelic Experience*. Blond 1966.

Maupoil, P., *La Géomancie à l'ancienne Côte des Esclaves*. Paris 1943.

Nicholson, R. A., *The Idea of Personality in Sūfism.* Cambridge 1923.

Nicholson, R. A., *Rūmī.* Allen & Unwin 1950.

O'Brien, E., *Varieties of Mystic Experience.* Mentor 1965.

Otto, R., *Mysticism East and West,* Meridian 1932.

Owen, H. P., 'Christian Mysticism' in *Religious Studies.* 1971.

Padwick, C., *Muslim Devotions.* S.P.C.K. 1961.

Paffard, M., *Inglorious Wordsworths.* Hodder 1973.

Panikkar, R., *The Unknown Christ of Hinduism.* Darton, Longman & Todd 1964.

Parrinder, E. G., *Avatar and Incarnation.* Faber 1970.

Parrinder, E. G., *West African Religion.* Epworth 1961 edn.

Parrinder, E. G., *Worship in the World's Religions.* Faber 1961, Sheldon 1974.

Plotinus, *Enneads,* tr. A. H. Armstrong. Penguin 1966.

Qur'ān, tr. R. Bell, T. & T. Clark 1937.

Rāmakrishna, Gospel of. New York 1942 edn.

Rawson, P., *The Art of Tantra.* Thames & Hudson 1973.

Rawson, P. and Legeza, L., *Tao.* Thames & Hudson 1973.

Reichelt, K., *Religion in Chinese Garment.* Lutterworth 1951.

Reyna, R., *The Concept of Māyā.* Asia Publishing House 1962.

Rig Veda, translated selections in R. C. Zaehner, *Hindu Scriptures.* Dent 1966.

Rolle, R., *The Fire of Love,* modernised by C. Wolters. Penguin 1972.

Sāmkhya Kārikā, tr. N. Sinha. Allahabad 1915.

Scharfstein, A., *Mystical Experience.* Thames & Hudson 1973.

Scholem, G. G., *Major Trends in Jewish Mysticism.* Thames & Hudson 1955.

Singh, T., ed., *Selections from the Sacred Writings of the Sikhs.* Allen & Unwin 1960.

Smart, N., *The Yogi and the Devotee.* Allen & Unwin 1968.

Smith, M., *Rābi 'a the Mystic.* Cambridge 1928.

Spiro, M., *Buddhism and Society.* Allen & Unwin 1971.

Stace, W. T., *Mysticism and Philosophy.* Macmillan 1960.

Suzuki, D. T., *Mysticism Christian and Buddhist.* Allen & Unwin 1957.

Tagore, D., *Autobiography.* Macmillan 1915.

SELECT BIBLIOGRAPHY

Tagore, R. *Gitanjali*. Macmillan 1913.

Tattvārthādhigama Sūtra, tr. J. L. Jaini. Arrah, India 1920.

Taylor, A. and Nilkanth, R. M., *Poems by Indian Women*. Calcutta 1923.

Teresa of Avila, *The Interior Castle*, tr. Sands 1945.

Traherne, T., *Centuries of Meditations*. Dobell 1934 edn.

Traherne, T., *Poems of Felicity*, Oxford 1910 edn.

Trimingham, J. S., *The Sufi Orders in Islam*. Oxford 1971.

Trimingham, J. S., *Two Worlds Are Ours*. Beirut 1971.

Tsunoda, R., ed., *Sources of Japanese Tradition*. Columbia 1958.

Udāna, tr. D. M. Strong. Luzac 1902.

Upanishads, tr. by R. E. Hume, *The Thirteen Principal Upanishads*. Oxford 1921; and R. C. Zaehner, *Hindu Scriptures*. Dent 1966.

Van Straelen, H., *The Religion of Divine Wisdom*, Tokyo 1954.

Vaudeville, C., *Kabīr*. Oxford 1974.

Vedānta Sūtras, tr. G. Thibaut. Oxford 1904.

Verger, P., *Notes sur le Culte des Orisa et Vodun*. Dakar 1957.

Waley, A., *The Analects of Confucius*. Allen & Unwin 1938.

Waley, A., *The Way and its Power*. Allen & Unwin 1934.

Watt, W. M., *The Faith and Practice of al-Ghazālī*. Allen & Unwin 1953.

Watt, W. M., *Muhammad at Mecca*. Oxford 1953.

Weber, M., *The Religion of India*. tr. Free Press, Illinois 1958.

Wesley, C. and J., in *The Methodist Hymn Book*. Epworth 1933.

Wilhelm, R. and Baynes, C. F., tr., *The Secret of the Golden Flower*. Routledge 1931.

Yoga Sūtras, tr. J. H. Wood in *The Yoga-system of Patañjali* 1914.

Zaehner, R. C., *At Sundry Times*. Faber 1958.

Zaehner, R. C., *The Bhagavad-Gītā*. Clarendon 1969.

Zaehner, R. C., *Drugs, Mysticism and Make-believe*. Collins 1972.

Zaehner, R. C., *Hindu and Muslim Mysticism*. Athlone Press 1960.

Zaehner, R. C., *Mysticism Sacred and Profane*. Clarendon Press 1957.

Zaehner, R. C.. *Our Savage God*. Collins 1974.

Zahan, D., ed., *Réincarnation et Vie Mystique en Afrique Noire*. Paris 1965.

Zohar, tr. Sperling, H., Simon, M. and Levertoff, P. Soncino 1931–4. Selections by G. G. Scholem, New York 1949.

INDEX

INDEX

Fremantle, A. 153, 200
Freud, S. 168, 170

Gautama, *see* Buddha
Ghazālī 129, 137f.
Ghose, Aurobindo 47f., 108, 200
Gilbert, W. S. 23
Gombrich, R. F. 54n., 59n., 63f., 200
gopīs, milkmaids 101
Gregory Nazianzen 147
Grierson, G. 106, 200
Guillaume, A. 122n., 125n., 167, 201
guru, teacher 105f., 108

Hāfiz 137
Hallāj, 14, 132, 135
Hardy, F. 102n., 201
Hare Krishna 3, 103, *and see* Krishna
Hasidism 118ff.
Herbert, G. 156
Herskovits, M. J. 83
Hesychasm 148
Hill, W. D. P. 92n, 104, 201
Hilton, W. 151, 187, 201
Hooper, J. S. M. 101n, 201
Hudson, W. H. 21f., 28f., 155, 201
Huxley, A. 13, 177ff., 183, 192, 201

Ibn 'Arabī 138f., 184
immanence, divine 35f., 95, 97, 107, 113, 115, 118, 125, 127, 141, 194, *and see* Monism *and* Pantheism
incarnation 135, 143

Iqbal, M. 140
Isaac, Syrian 148
Islam 121ff., 141
isolation 45, 51
Īśvara Gītā 106

Jacobs, L. 118, 201
Jains 43, 49ff., 57, 161
James, W. 16, 176f., 201
Jayadeva 100
Jefferies, R. 28
Jesus Christ 24, 135ff., 142ff., 148f., 151ff., 165ff., 171, 185ff., 191f., 194
Joan of Arc 24, 125
John XXIII 183
John of Cross 152f., 166, 201
Joseph, B. 112
Judaism 114ff., 141
Julian of Norwich 151f., 171, 201
Junayd 134f., 184

Kabīr 104ff., 172
karma 50, 57, 93
Keble, J. 160
Kern, H. 62n., 201
Keyt, G. 100, 201
Khayyām, Omar 137
Klostermaier, K. 103, 201
Koran *see* Qur'ān
Krishna 3, 15, 38, 94f., 99ff., 105, 114, 171f.

Lallā 106, 200
Lamb, C. 156
Landau, R. 138, 201
Laski, M. 21, 201

INDEX